All lives changed by God's p ᴛy
estimation), but Floyd's deserve ᴜu
for telling your story with humi. ᴉ I
thank God that you have a proven testimony over many
years.

Don Wilkerson
Co-Founder of Teen Challenge & Times Square Church

The tradition of changed lives and success stories from
Teen Challenge—from David Wilkerson's *The Cross and
the Switchblade* to Nicki Cruz's *Run Baby Run*—
continues with the Floyd Miles III in *Harlem Is Where I
Began.* I've known Floyd for many years and can attest
that he is the real deal. I've heard many of these stories
before and am thrilled that they are finally making it to a
wider audience. The accounts are thrilling, informative,
and inspirational. Once you start reading, you'll find it hard
to put down! Jesus is still changing lives today!

Joe Paskewich
Pastor of Calvary Chapel in Eastern Connecticut

I have had the joy of knowing Floyd Miles for more than 20
years now and can say without reservation that I am proud
of Floyd's faithfulness to the call of God on his life.

Hundreds of people have been directly impacted by Floyd's testimony and counsel. In this book, you will hear a story of the power of the grace of God. When I think of all the challenges Floyd faced as a young man in a tough neighborhood and the loss of his parents, I'm reminded that God's grace is truly amazing. Floyd had every excuse and opportunity to destroy his life and to give up on hope. But, he didn't. He said yes to hope when he walked through the doors of Teen Challenge and remained open to God's voice throughout his life. That is why he is so effective in speaking truth into the lives of others. Floyd pursued higher education and completed undergraduate and masters degrees, which speaks volumes about his desire to learn and to be effective in his role as a leader. I pray that everyone who reads this book will appreciate Floyd's commitment to his faith, his family, and to leading with excellence.

Jerry Nance, PhD
President, Global Teen Challenge

"Amazing grace, how sweet the sound..." Rev. Floyd Miles III story is a living testimony of God's grace. I recommend him, his ministry, and this grace filled book.

Bishop Walter Harvey
President, Nat'l Black Fellowship of the Assemblies of God

Floyd Miles III is on my short list of people to call when I need perspective regarding racial and cultural issues. I first met Floyd over thirty years ago at a Teen Challenge national conference. Floyd impressed me with his meek and soft-spoken manner that also showed strength through a powerful voice when he shared his convictions. He is still of the same character today. Floyd's book will inspire you as he tells his story of redemption, cultural insights, and ministry leadership.

Randy Rowe, PhD
CEO, Teen Challenge NorWestCal Nevada

Floyd's journey classically depicts God's grace—for an individual and an entire family. It also pictures a resolve and commitment to follow Christ, as a response to the hope and freedom given. Floyd mirrors Christ the same with his family and his neighbors, as when he serves his church or at Adult & Teen Challenge. I'm honored to serve alongside Floyd and believe he'll need to add more chapters to this journey because our greatest years of ministry still lie ahead of us!

George M. Thomas, M.B.A., DMin
President/CEO, Adult & Teen Challenge of Texas

Rev. Floyd A. Miles III is a servant of God whose life and testimony God's transforming power has inspired many. The Kingdom of God has a General in him and you will certainly be blessed by this book.

Rev. Dr. John Aniemeke, **Lead Pastor Bethel Covenant Assembly of God, San Antonio**

What a joy and privilege it is for me to have known Pastor Floyd for more than 30 years. I admire his successful journey, using negative challenge as stepping stones instead of stumbling blocks. Pastor Floyd has a unique spirit of determination and very few people I know can match his sincerity. I highly recommended book.

Bishop Spencer Jones
People United to Save Urban America

Floyd has accomplished many wonderful things; being faithful to the call of God being the greatest. God has allowed him to achieve many of the dreams his father never got a chance to do. I'm very proud of Floyd as a son and a man of God, a living epistle before his family and friends and the Teen Challenge Community, nationally and internationally.

Barbara Miles
Floyd's Proud Step-Mom

HARLEM

IS WHERE I BEGAN

THE JOURNEY OF FLOYD A. MILES III

CONTENTS

DEDICATION

I dedicate this book to my Lord and Savior, Jesus Christ, my wife, my mother, father, grandmother(s), grandfather(s), my children, grandchildren, great grandchildren and beyond!

Also, I dedicate this book to the rest of my family, Adult & Teen Challenge, my friend Rev. Joe Paskewich, the late Rev. Dr. John Q. Kenzy, my Pastors Rev. Dr. John and Chidi Aniemeke and the countless others whom God has used to pray for me and help me on my journey.

FOREWORD

Some years ago I was speaking at a conference and I looked out on the audience into a sea of white faces. There in the midst was Floyd, one of the few African Americans in the crowd. The conference was about reaching drug addicts through the faith-based approach. At the time, I felt a strong urge that there should be greater efforts made in reaching more African American addicts. This book is intended to be one small step in that needed direction.

I have known Floyd for years—when he was at his worse and, by God's grace, when he was at his best. He always and wholeheartedly gives God all the glory. Floyd's life in Harlem was promising, yet very messy as he grew older. By sheer determination and faith in God, he made something of himself, looking for role models wherever he could find them. I saw his father come to faith in Christ out of a life of addiction and then live a stable and successful life—and Floyd echoed his journey of faith in achieving the same. His life transformation gives hope to all addicts, but especially to those like himself. All lives changed by God's power are miracles (in my estimation), but Floyd's deserves special notice because he's a product of Harlem and the black community.

It's my prayer that this book can prompt a discussion of how to increase outreach evangelism to drug addicts and alcoholics everywhere—but especially among African Americans, beginning in Harlem and beyond. Floyd, thank you for telling your story with humility and raw honesty, and I thank God that you have a proven testimony over many years.

—*Rev. Don Wilkerson*
Co-Founder of Teen Challenge & Times Square Church

INTRODUCTION

I'd like to share with you the story of my life (so far) for various reasons:

- To offer hope to those struggling with drug abuse, addiction, and any other life-controlling problem,

- So that people who possess a very limited knowledge of Jesus Christ can come to personally and intimately know more of His love, goodness, mercy and grace,

- To inspire and provoke current and future Teen Challenge students and graduates to strive for excellence, and allow God to accomplish greater things in their lives than past graduates (like myself),

- And that my family would know: all that is good in our lineage can be attributed fully to God. Had He not divinely intervened in our affairs, we would be spiritually poor(er) souls.

- FYI—even if you don't fall into any of the four groups mentioned above, by God's grace, my hope and prayer is that you too can find hope and inspiration from my personal journey, one which began in the heart of Central Harlem.

Floyd A. Miles III

1
The Heart of Harlem

I grew up in the heart of Harlem. No matter where I have gone since, Harlem has always stayed in my heart and my soul. Harlem is the most famous and one of the largest African American neighborhoods in the United States. Even before its recent gentrification, there has always been a unique mixture of ethnicities and cultures, each with its own particular style of music, clothing, food and artistic talents; actually, talents of all kinds! Just by walking down any given Harlem avenue you will run across a wide variety of stores and people and items for sale. There are many churches and businesses, sights and sounds, smiles and scents. If New York city is a melting pot, then Harlem is a hand-sewn, multi-colored quilt. It is not a museum-piece quilt, for sure, but rather one that is well used and worn and, yes, dirty and torn in places.

On trips back from New Jersey and elsewhere, when getting off the A Train at my stop (125th street) when I arrived up the stairs, I distinctly remember deeply breathing in that unique Harlem air. I welcomed and looked forward to it. Just like Dorothy in *The Wizard of Oz*, I would say to myself, *"There's no place like home!"* Listen to the range of emotions and various reflections from some famous quotes about Harlem (or from Harlemites):

Harlem is a stage. It is like its own planet; from the way we dress to the swag in the way we walk and talk.[i]

—Teyana (Singer-Songwriter)

Despite everything that Harlem did to our generation, I think it gave something to a few. It gave them a strength that couldn't be obtained anywhere else.[ii]

—Claude Brown
(Author of *Manchild in the Promised Land*)

I gained an appreciation of the Harlem Renaissance, a time when African Americans rose to prominence in American culture. For the first time, they were taken seriously as artists, musicians, writers, athletes, and political thinkers.[iii]

—Kareem Abdul-Jabbar (Hall of Fame NBA player)

Harlem is filled with moments of history.[iv]

—Cheo Hodari Coker (Television Writer and Producer)

Crisis' seems to be too mild a word to describe conditions in countless African American communities. It is beyond crisis when in the richest nation in the world, African Americans in Harlem live shorter lives than the people of Bangladesh, one of the poorest nations of the world.[v]

—Johnnetta B. Cole (Anthropologist, Museum Director and College President)

A man who stands for nothing will fall for anything...We want one thing. We declare our right on this earth to be a man, to be a human being, to be respected as a human being, to be given the rights of a human being in this society, on this earth, in this day, which we intend to bring into existence by any means necessary.[vi]

—Malcolm X (Civil Rights Leader)

Harlem was home, was where we belonged; where we knew and were known in return; where we felt most alive; where, if need be, somebody had to take us in. Harlem defined us, claiming our consciousness and, I suspect, our unconsciousness.[vii]

—Ossie Davis (Actor, Director, Poet & Civil Rights Activist)

I was born in Harlem, raised in the South Bronx, went to public school, got out of public college, went into the Army, and then I just stuck with it.[viii]

—Colin Powell (Politician, Diplomat and Retired Four-Star General)

Many people in Harlem never go out of Harlem. I mean they'd never even been downtown. And you can see how this bitterness can accumulate. Here you see people crowded and hovered up in ghettos and slums with no hope. They see no way out.[ix]

—Martin Luther King, Jr. (Civil Rights Leader)

Hurry, get on board, it's coming', Listen to those rails a-thrumming, All aboard. Get on the "A" train, Soon you will be on Sugar Hill in Harlem.[x]

—Duke Ellington (Composer, Jazz Orchestra Leader)

Can you hear the multitude of voices in this song we call Harlem: *the swag, the strength, the renaissance, the artists, the political thinkers, the crisis', the injustices, the bitterness and the heartfelt, continuous singing?*

This awesome and harsh world called Harlem is where I was born. I was blessed to live a few blocks away from the Abyssinian Baptist Church, where Harlem Congressman Adam Clayton Powell, Jr. pastored for 34 years. Abyssinian Baptist Church was the first African American Baptist Church in the state of New York. Rev. Wyatt Tee Walker pastored Canaan Baptist Church on 116th Street between Seventh and Lenox Avenues. He had been the Chief of Staff for Martin Luther King, Jr. It is hard for me to believe that I once walked into his church under

14

the influence of drugs and announced that I wanted to be a minister. I did the same thing at the Union Theological Seminary once, located on Broadway at Columbia University. Both times, I was promptly escorted out. Perhaps they would have helped me had I not been high on drugs!

I also lived just one block from the famous Apollo Theater on 125th Street. Author Ted Fox has said, *"The Apollo has probably exerted a greater influence on popular culture than any other entertainment venue in the world."*[xi] As a kid, I would walk past that landmark, reading the famous names up there in lights, displayed on the marquees. I got to see virtually every popular R&B/soul singer there during the 1960's and 70's. As you might imagine, I was not a paying customer. I snuck in with my friends.

Without question, James Brown, AKA Soul Brother #1, the Godfather of soul and the hardest working man in show business, was the most popular act by a landslide. When he came to town, the line easily tripled in length, and inside the Apollo Theater there was standing room only.

This could have been a magical world to grow up in if I had not been so spiritually blind. Although there were some good traits about me—positive aspirations and latent talents—this blindness caused me to make horrible choices growing up. I really wasn't a very bad person, but I did some pretty bad things. Growing up, I went to church. At times, I was even a bit active in church. My sister, two cousins and I all got baptized in water. However, this was just a ritual to me. It was supposed to mean something according to the Word of God, but it did not do anything. Or, should I say, *I* did not do anything? All that happened was, I went down into the water a dry sinner and came up a wet sinner. That was the gist of it. Once again, although I was not a notorious fellow, I was doing bad things. I had not really surrendered my life to Jesus.

Without a trace of bitterness, I must also add that I was born with two strikes against me: the sad condition of my lost and wayward father and the even sadder condition of my dear mother.

*   *   *   *   *

I remember playing in my elementary schoolyard with my grade school friends when one of them nudged me. "That man outside the fence. He's staring at you, Floyd."

Turning, I looked at the rusted chain link barrier that surrounded our play area, protecting us from the rough people that roamed the Harlem streets. Sure enough, the man at the fence was staring right at me. His clothes were wrinkled and dirty; his face was so downcast. But my heart leaped. I knew it was my Dad and I ran toward the fence.

When he saw me coming, the man turned and ran off down the sidewalk.

"Daddy!" I shouted after him when I reached the fence. "Daddy, come back!" But he hustled down the block and disappeared around a corner into the jungle of concrete surrounding us.

My fingers gripped the chain links as hot tears came to my eyes. "Hey, Floyd," my friends called. But I couldn't turn around and let them see me crying like a little baby. I gripped the fence harder as my heart tried to race after the daddy who couldn't even look me in the face or talk to me. He was on one of his binges. Right at that moment, that rusted fence was one of the few solid things I could hold on to in my tattered life.

My father and mother both were heroin addicts. I hold no malice or bitterness towards my parents for their drug use. I never have taken their negligence personal. In hindsight, because of my own drug use, I now can see that they just did not have the coping skills to be good parents. Also, I'm sure that when they first started using drugs, they did not set out to become addicts. I know that was not in my plans either; but it happened! The pleasure that I got from the drugs seduced me!

Although, I never shot heroin into my veins like my mom and dad, I am reminded of these tragic words, part of a twisted rewording of the beloved 23rd Psalm, discovered years ago in Reidsville, North Carolina in a closed car alongside a dead heroin addict. She was 23 years old and her death was ruled a suicide. A hookup with the car's exhaust had sent carbon monoxide fumes from a running motor into her vehicle. I wish it were not as timely today, but sadly, it may be even more so. Here's the complete "Psalm."

King Heroin Is My Shepherd

King Heroin is my shepherd; I shall always want.

He maketh me to lie down in the gutter, he leadeth me beside the troubled waters, he destroyeth my soul.
He leadeth me in the paths of wickedness.

Yea, I shall walk through the valley of poverty and will fear no evil, for thou, Heroin, are with me.
Thy needle and capsule comfort me.

Thou strippest the table of groceries in the presence of my family. Thou robbest my head of reason.
My cup of sorrow runneth over.

Surely heroin addiction shall stalk me all the days of my life and I will dwell in the House of the Damned forever.[xii]

Also found in the car with the dead woman was this written message: *"Jail didn't cure me. Nor did hospitalization help me for long. The doctors told my family it would have been better and kinder if the person who got me hooked on dope had taken a gun and blown my brains out. And I wish to God he had. My God, how I wish it!"*

Over the years, in counseling people who have struggled with drugs and had parents who were addicts, I've asked them if they could try to forgive and be more understanding of their parent's addiction, their behavior, and for not rearing them properly. If possible, I try to let them see that their parent's negligence wasn't intentional and that they were spiritually lost. Also, if they have become "born again" Christians, I try to get them to see how the drugs caused them to do the same thing that their parent had done. However, if God forgave and didn't judge them, they should try to do the same. This makes sense.

Let me give an example: Years ago a student in the Teen Challenge Program who was a new believer in Jesus Christ became livid when he found out for the first time that all the while when his dad was traveling south to find work when he was a little boy, he was cheating on his mom and was living with another woman. Because this had devastated his mom, he wanted to do bodily harm to his dad. I understood his anger and disappointment in his dad.

However, over the course of several meetings with him, I was able to show him that prior to his giving his heart to the Lord he was "chasing skirts" all over the state and cheating on his own wife. I explained to him that he and his dad were acting like many (not all) unsaved men all over the world. I was able to show him that he should lighten up a little bit on his dad just because—as they say—when you point one finger at someone, three fingers are point back at you.

* * * * *

My mother's name was Vivian Naomi Miles, but they called her by her middle name or her nickname, Na. Na is my youngest daughter's nickname, also. Her full name in Jea'na, a combination of her maternal mother's name "Norma Jean" and my mother "Naomi." My mom met my father when she was about fourteen years old. Floyd, Jr. was 22 years old and at the time was running the streets and getting high. He had already had several jail stints by the time they started hanging out in the neighborhood. My father was introduced to my mother by a mutual friend named Turk. Naomi was just a girl Floyd saw hanging around the neighborhood. But one day at Turk's apartment, my father noticed her, and there was an instant connection between them. He noticed a sort of sparkle and fun-loving way about Naomi with a light in her eyes.

20

My mother's sparkle attracted other people, as well. She was petite in size at five-foot-one and was soft-spoken and humble. She always wore her hair short and it framed her face nicely. Since Naomi was my grandmother's child, she and her younger sister (my Aunt Joyce) was raised to be active in the church and even sang in the young adult choir. There must have been something unique about my mother's quiet nature that also complimented her outgoing spirit because my father was attracted to it right away.

Floyd, Jr. remembers asking Turk, *"She use dope?"* Turk said no, and my dad smiled, relieved to know she wasn't an addict like him. From that day on, my father called Nay, *"his girl."* They would run the streets together for several years, eventually getting married and trying their best to be a father and mother to my sister Denise and me. Later, my parents separated. My father spent most of his time out on the streets feeding his heroin addiction, and my mother moved out of my Grandmother Nina's place into another apartment. She moved on to other boyfriends and even asked my father for a divorce. He agreed, but they never went through with it and remained close friends.

My father was allowed to take me to see his side of the family on his good days when I was little. My grandmother would allow this. To one of his sisters, my dad was very close. Her name was Mary and she lived in the Bronx. I liked going over to my Aunt Mary's house. Sometimes me, my sister, and two cousins would spend the night there. After my dad made our rounds to see his family, he would take the little money from me that they would give me before returning me to my grandmother. They gave me the money because they did not see me often and wanted to bless me in some way.

My maternal grandmother and my Aunt Joyce were my primary caretakers even though my mother would visit me from time to time. When I did see her, she would stop by for a while, and then tell me she had to leave to go to the grocery store for milk, cookies, or some other item. She would not come back until about two or three days later. I never knew where she went or when she would return. Nevertheless, regardless of how long she would be gone, when she did return, she would bring milk or cookies, as promised. My mother never nurtured me, but even in those simple promises of milk and cookies, she somehow conveyed to me that she cared and loved me...until she was gone permanently.

Some people are bitter and feel abandoned by their parents. I understand; and God understands. However, when my dad did eventually surrender his heart to the Lord, I did not love him any more than I did when he used heroin. I truly loved him unconditionally, even when I was a child. God loves us unconditionally, too. He doesn't say,

"Clean yourself up and then come to Me." He says, *"Come to me and I will clean you up."*

2

The Infamous Sunday Picnic

After church one Sunday, we headed home to get ready for a picnic in the park. It's hard to recall all the details, but I do remember being excited, like any rambunctious boy would be. My grandmother and Aunt Joyce (my mother's younger sister) were preparing all the food for our big lunch. Glenda (my first cousin) and I were running around the apartment with excitement. It was going to be a family outing with Nina, Aunt Joyce, my first cousins Rennie and Glenda. Janice, a little girl from next door and her brother Michael was also invited to our picnic. My sister Denise, who was one year older than me, was not there.

Unfortunately, Denise and I grew up separated from each other. She lived with my Aunt Lucy, my grandmother's oldest sister. Thankfully, my sister and I did see each other often. She would come and stay with us for short periods. However, it was a far cry from us bonding like true brothers and sisters do. We've always had a deep love for each other, though. Understandably, she resented living separated from me. Although she did not want for anything and was surrounded by love, she lived in a one-bedroom apartment alone with our Aunt Lucy, who was well into her 60's when

Denise moved in with her at birth as a heroin addicted baby from Harlem Hospital. I, on the other hand, was situated in the midst of a family.

I can imagine that growing up, my sister would wonder what was wrong with her and why we were not together. Thankfully, the Lord healed her of the hurt that she experienced from this after her conversion to Christianity in the 90's. God delivered her from selling and using drugs. Whenever I think about my sister's conversion, I'm reminded of the saying: *"He (God) may not come when you want Him to, but He's always on time."* What do I mean? Well, around that time, I was down because I felt that although my family was happy for me that I had turned my life around, I was not seeing any spiritual progress in them as a whole. Generally, it seemed to me that some of my family's attitudes towards me was that I needed Jesus. I was the one who was doing crazy things. However, finding religion to the degree that I did, wasn't necessary for them. It was during the holiday season, while laying on my bed with tears streaming down my face, I asked the Lord to move in my family.

Shortly after that prayer, I received a call from my sister. I remember her simply saying to me that she was ready! I took her to Teen Challenge. In her personal testimony, she tells how she was about to put a gun to her head before crying out for help. Today, she is an evangelist!

We both have hearts to help people who were just like us! Back to the day of the picnic...

"Nay, you coming?" I heard Nina ask while I was in the other room. I listened to her muffled voice as she answered. As we all headed out the door, I learned my mother wasn't coming. I looked back at her, resting on the red sofa with white doilies on it. Those doilies served two purposes: they were decorative and they also hid the cigarette burns on the fabric. She was lying down with her head against one of those doilies. I wasn't quite sure why my mother wasn't coming, but I figured she probably wasn't feeling well, again.

It was perfect weather for a picnic along the Hudson River. That particular day it was unseasonably cooler than most mid-August afternoons in New York City. It would be a great day to relax, play, eat and enjoy the sunshine without the usual sweltering heat of summer. We drove to the park and set up our picnic area. Riverside Park borders Upper Manhattan along the Hudson River. You could look west across the river to New Jersey or spot the expansive George Washington Bridge up north a little ways.

We soon finished our picnic lunch, and as we played, the neighbor girl Janice somehow managed to get her socks wet. Nina told her to take them off, and my grandmother placed them on the grill that was cooling down. Glenda and

I laughed at the sight of two white socks cooking on the grill.

All of the sudden a yellow taxi cab pulled up nearby and my mother's boyfriend, Robert, jumped out of the car. He ran toward Nina and with a panicked voice said, "Come quickly! Something's wrong with Nay." Immediately I remember feeling the fear and anxiety coming from all the adults. Our picnic was cut short and Nina quickly left with Robert in the cab.

I was only five years old. My birthday was coming up the next month in September. I'll never forget that August afternoon. A day that started with anticipation and sunshine and happiness turned to complete mayhem. The adults tried their best to shield us from the tragedy. I remember we weren't allowed to go back into our apartment for a long time. We waited for what seemed like hours before we could return home. The long wait stirred up more anxious thoughts and fears that the adults were unsuccessfully trying to shield us from.

August 11th, 1963 was the day my sister Denise and I lost our mother, Naomi Vivian Miles. My grandmother lost her firstborn daughter. Naomi died in our home on my grandmother's bed; the same apartment where my grandmother raised her and the same place she said her wedding vows with my father. That last gaze of my mother lying on the red sofa was the last time I would see her dear face.

They told me she died of a heart attack. I would somewhat believe that lie up until I was a young adult. I would question it privately because heart disease did not run in our family. But I wasn't allowed to ask questions surrounding my mother's death. It was too painful for Nina. It was secretive, and a family matter better left untold. Maybe they were shielding me from pain? Perhaps they were protecting the beautiful sparkle that was my mother's nature when she was healthy and clean. The harsh reality was that my mother died of a heroin overdose. She was only twenty-eight years old.

Many years later I discovered the truth surrounding her untimely death, and I was told by my godfather that she had overdosed from heroin; like I had always suspected. It's funny that even though I suspected that my mother died from heroin for so long, I still grieved when I found out. I remember after being told the truth that I laid across my bed. I didn't usually cry much, but tears did roll down my eyes and I felt so empty inside. Before getting up off of the bed, I vowed to God that I would continue helping young and old alike get off drugs and find hope and eternal life in Jesus Christ. I didn't want any child whose mother or father was in the Teen Challenge program where I was then serving at in Brockton, Massachusetts to die from a drug overdose or be killed.

Regarding my mother's death, I had an important conversation years later with my granddad's brother, Hubert Reaves. He was the Senior Pastor of a church I visited with the men from Teen Challenge. We were there to present the ministry. The church was located in the Bronx. It was the first time I met him and he told me an interesting story about my mother. He said the day before she died, Mom visited with her father—my grandfather—Jasper Reaves. They had a long conversation in the church office where he was pastoring at the time. Shortly after that, my mom had the tragic accident and overdosed from heroin. The way I look at what Hubert told me is: I don't know what my mom and my granddad talked about, but the timing of their conversation always gives me hope. This is what I figure: my grandfather Jasper was a minister of the gospel and his daughter was hurting. She was a drug addict who needed help. A pastor's discussion in a church office should always include a time of prayer. Did he lead her in the sinner's prayer? Did my mother accept the Lord into her heart the day before she died?

I don't know the answers to my questions and I'm not a betting man. However, if I were, I'd bet that my mother poured her heart out to her dad about how her life was so messed up and how she needed help. And, I believe that my granddaddy held his daughter's hands, looked her in the eyes and, like he's said so many times before, he lovingly told her that he'd do anything in the world for her; but that what she really needed to do was to surrender her life to Jesus. Yes, I want to believe that in spite of my mom's tragic accident, that in that church office with her being in there only with her earthly father (my granddad) and her heavenly Father (God), she gave her heart to Jesus Christ. Then, I believe that my granddaddy gave her a long, big hug before my mom left the church. Of course I can't prove any of this, but I'm believing that my mom made things right with the Lord. When I enter heaven, the first person I'm going to look for is my beautiful, petite, quiet-natured mother. I'll look for her in the crowd and ask to sit down with her. Who knows, maybe we'll even be able to enjoy some milk and cookies together.

3
The Unsung Heroes of Harlem

Surely the unsung heroes, at least in Harlem, are the grandmothers who—because of a host of reasons and situations—find themselves raising their dear grandkids, doing the very best they can, sometimes in very hard circumstances. My grandmother Nina, as we affectionately called her, was a proud woman, raising her family at 2137 Seventh Avenue, Apartment 5, between 126th and 127th Streets. Surely this was the heart of Harlem, with the famous Apollo Theater just two blocks around the corner. Influential Harlem Renaissance artists and musicians had previously walked along the same sidewalks that bordered my tenement building. Famous jazz performers from the 1920's and later would come shuffling by along Seventh Avenue. But to be somebody—according to Nina—meant you also had to get your feet to church every single Sunday.

Mattie Reaves, aka Ma Mattie by her church friends and Nina (pronounced with a long "I") by her grandchildren was a Christian woman who believed going to church was first, no matter what events took place later on that day and the week to come. Nina would often nudge me to quiet down with a stern stare that seemed to say, "Stop all that squirming, Floyd!" My grandmother was a devout church

31

lady who always dressed the part in her pristine clothes and fancy feathered hats. She was a praying woman, and like my cousin Glenda would say, "Nina has a way with Jesus. He *is* her Lord." Everyone in the family knew that Nina was committed to church attendance, prayer, teaching Sunday school, singing in the choir, cooking in the church kitchen, assisting the pastor and visiting the sick and shut in. She deeply loved the Lord.

My grandmother was born in Windsor, North Carolina on February 6th, 1906. By the time I came along, she was divorced from my grandfather, Jasper Reaves. They had two daughters: Vivian Naomi Reaves (my mom) and her younger sister, Joyce. Also, I would learn when my Aunt Joyce passed away that my grandmother had a son. His name was Stew Lee. He had travelled from Windsor, North Carolina to attend his sister's funeral. Apparently, this was another one of the family's secrets.

I vaguely remember my grandfather, who was a Baptist minister and at one time served on the pastoral staff at Mt. Moriah Baptist Church, located at 20-50 5th Avenue, between 126th and 127th Street. This was our home church. There were only a few times I remember him coming around. When he did, he usually brought us some food. One time he delivered live chickens to us. Those chickens would run around our third-floor apartment. Of course, to eat them, someone would have to break their necks first. I'll never forget watching a chicken get its head pulled off while still running around half-alive on the apartment floor. After witnessing that peculiar scene, my Aunt Joyce couldn't find it in herself to eat that chicken, no matter how good it might have tasted.

Just like my mother's death and my grandmother having a son, my grandparents' divorce was not a subject of discussion. It was taboo to ask questions or even to talk about it. As I grew older, I discovered there were a few family topics that were not allowed to be spoken of or questioned amongst family members. To be honest, I've had the sense for many years that something went terribly wrong in my family after my grandparent's divorce. Their break-up seemed to open the door to more and more heartache and to cause things to "scatter" in so many of our lives.

Nina was a hardworking single mother raising her two daughters in Harlem. She worked as a laundry presser and would travel downtown each weekday to the East Side of Manhattan to work at a Jewish-owned dry cleaner. When Nina wasn't working, she was most likely at church or helping in the soup kitchen. Nina was a giver who gave of herself in so many ways, including to her family. It was her faith in God, her commitment to her family, and her hard work that were her most important legacies left to me.

There were other heroes in Harlem as I was growing up; some unsung and some very famous ones. Our country was filled with turmoil and change during the 1960's. The two main things I recall is the unrest surrounding the Vietnam War and the growing Civil Rights Movement. In the heart of central Harlem—like in every other black community around the country—black people were in an uproar because they wanted equality, justice and freedom.

One of my closest friends' parents owned a small but prominent black bookstore known all over the world. The African National Memorial Bookstore was originally located between 125th and 126th Streets on Seventh Avenue. Lewis Michaux Sr., the owner, was also a civil rights activist. Malcolm X spoke on a stage right outside of this store on a number of occasions. During this time, virtually every black politician, dignitary and/or ambassador from other countries came to this store when they visited Harlem. I saw Malcolm X there when I was eight years old. That was also the year he was killed in Harlem at the Audubon Ballroom.

The Black Panthers headquarters was on Seventh Avenue, going towards Central Park. I remember they had a lot of programs that helped the youth in our community. If I were to be perfectly honest, I took Malcolm X's famous saying "…by any means necessary" and the Black Panther's stance of "demanding" freedom, equality, justice and respect the same way that the American patriot Patrick Henry did when war against Great Britain was looming. He famously declared, "I know not what course others may take; but as for me, give me liberty or give me death!"

Also in Harlem, there was a pseudo-Muslim group called the Five Percenters that did many things to help the youth, as well. Their headquarters was also on Seventh Avenue, between 126th and 127th Streets, directly across the street from where I lived. Today, that building is still there. To many of the residents of Harlem, they were heroes who were doing good. However, people who did not live in Harlem did not feel this way.

I'm extremely grateful for all the civil rights activists of that day, (in the north and the south) e.g., Dr. Martin Luther King, Jr., Coretta Scott King, Thurgood Marshall, Adam Clayton Powell, Jr., Chaney, Goodman and Schwerner (activists in Mississippi who gave their lives), Medgar Evers, Fannie Lou Hamer, Rosa Parks, John Lewis, James Farmer, Whitney Young, Jr., Mamie Till Mosley, Andrew Young, John Lewis, etc., etc. I recognize that today, I am standing on their proverbial shoulders.

To this very day, Martin Luther King, Jr. is one of my most endeared heroes. I remember standing outside of the record shop, listening to his speeches. They were so inspiring. For years, while serving in Teen Challenge, every MLK, Jr. Day, I would gather all the students together (red, yellow, black and white) and we'd listen to his most famous speeches. Then we'd have discussed how our gathering was the fulfillment of Dr. King's dream. Also, I remember my Aunt Joyce made all of us stay home for school in order to watch his funeral. I remember the riots, particularly the ones when Dr. King was assassinated. I was in the bookstore that my friend's father owned. His mother had sensed that things would happen and told me and my cousin to quickly go home. We only lived one block away. However, we still got caught in the street when the people's anger and frustration exploded like a thousand hand grenades. I was only eleven years old. However, I was what I would call a New York "eleven". This meant that I was very street savvy. When I left the shop, I saw that some people were trying to get into a jewelry store, so I detoured and decided to try my luck at getting some items. However, when a police officer hit me across my butt with his Billy club, that was my sign to go home!

Unfortunately, just like in the sixties, today many angry and fed up black people are rioting in our cities. I understand their frustrations and have felt their pain. There are some instances where I still do! However, while it does get the attention of the media and it makes a powerful statement, there are a number of reasons why I personally think it is not the best strategy for change. Just to name a few: it works against the efforts in the black community; it hurts a lot of businesses and people who have done no wrong; and it does not solve the root causes of the problems. Also, it is a known fact that professional agitators go to cities and participate in the destruction. There's a better way!

I remember when we would go downtown to the movies and we'd dress up because it was a big deal. But I could feel the racism. The feeling I got from some people who looked at me was that I belonged uptown. What was I doing down here? Then, of course, there was my always being followed in the stores whenever I was downtown. This still happens today, although I am not a shoplifter!

In school however, I never did experience any racism. When I was in an all-black school, they loved on us and wanted the best for us. They understood what a typical black household was like. Not all of them, though. I think this is the assumption that a lot of people make...that all black people are poor, lazy, on drugs, don't read, etc. That is so far from the truth. In Harlem (and in any community, for that matter) there are both good and bad people. However, prejudice is just that...pre judging people. My grandmother taught us that just because the neighborhood someone lives in is bad, doesn't mean that the person is bad.

Things being what they were at home, I'd have to say I got my education on the streets. When I was around eleven, I started working at odd jobs—sweeping up a barbershop, stocking shelves in a grocery store, working in a record shop, working in a candy store, and running errands for people. People took a liking to me. Maybe it was because I didn't have a mother or a father. Somehow there was always an older person who at least pointed out what I needed to do and helped keep me out of serious trouble. Oftentimes, even if the older person was not doing the right thing themselves, they would try to steer me in the right direction. If I am perfectly honest, I will have to say that it is an absolute miracle from God that I never came close to being sexually abused or physically assaulted.

My job at Mr. Jimmy's Barber Shop was to sweep the floor and the sidewalk outside. The Hall of Fame basketball player Kareem Abdul Jabber came down the block one time. He didn't say anything to us kids, though. Do you remember grandpa from "The Munsters?" He even passed through my block. That was strange seeing him! I once saw Louie Armstrong come into the barber shop to get a manicure. Whoever said that men did not gossip was wrong. In that shop the men would passionately talk about anything and everything. Some of the things I remember hearing being discussed were: women, sports, gambling, headline news, arts and entertainment, the neighborhood happenings, and politics. I got much of my "education and street smarts" from working in the barber shop and hanging around gambling and after hour spots, or just standing around, hanging out on the street corners.

4

A Kid With Promise

The first elementary school I attended was PS. 68 (Public School Number 68), located on 127th Street, between Seventh and Lenox Avenues. (Now Seventh Avenue is called Adam Clayton Powell Blvd. and Lenox Avenue is called Malcom X Blvd. In the early days, this was not the case.) When I was in the fourth grade, the Harlem school system had identified me and some other kids as having "promise." A bunch of us were transferred to another school (PS. 125) and put in a track for the intelligent and gifted. In the first elementary school I attended the students were mostly African American. However, this other school, P.S. 125, (where I was transferred to attend the IGC classes—intelligently gifted children) was multi-racial. I remember there were Mexicans, Puerto Ricans, Chinese, Whites and Japanese kids in my 5th grade class. This I thought was cool and I really enjoyed it. However, even before being transferred, I had not allowed myself to get contaminated with prejudice.

The evening my grandmother and I took the city bus to my new school for orientation, I was so excited. What would it be like to be in a new school with better equipment and with kids of different races? It felt like a whole new world opening up for me. Someone thought I had *promise* and that I was *gifted*.

All the other kids' parents were eager, alert and asking questions. And right in the middle of it all, as we sat in the very front seats, my grandma—a hardworking, tired lady—fell sound asleep. Everyone around us could hear her loud breathing, and I could have died of embarrassment.

In 1973 my aunt died. She had tried to help raise me and her two children the best way she could. So now the little bit of discipline I'd had was gone. My aunt had been a heavy drinker. Her blood pressure had always run high, and drinking didn't help her cause one bit. Now Grandma was left to raise us three kids on her own. To put it that way, though, is a joke. With everything resting on her shoulders, all she could do, literally, was work to keep her mind, body and soul together. The laundry consumed long daytime shifts. And church was the only comfort and encouragement for the soul of a sweet, strong woman who had outlived her own daughters. Beyond that, we really were on our own. Now, more and more, the streets were becoming my home.

In my new school, my music class wanted me to play the cello. I told them, "No way, Jose! That's for sissies and squares." I wanted to be super cool and would only play the drums or guitar; and maybe the piano. I dropped out of that class because they said no to my demands. That was a big mistake on my part. Today, I'm around a lot of musicians who I see enjoying what they do. Some of them even make a lot of money. I blew a great opportunity.

So many bad mistakes were made by me because I just wanted to be cool and I had no real, strong, parental supervision. I didn't have any boundaries, either. As long as I was not violent or hurting anyone, I could almost do anything I wanted. The nerdy kids (or shall I say, the kids with more discipline and structure) went home much earlier than me. I used to laugh and tease them. In hindsight, they had it right. I did not, even though I was "so called" cool and I was making money hustling on the streets. There's a saying that "You should never laugh and make fun of a nerd. Why? Because you might wind up working for one!"

Naturally, my grades began to go down because I was no longer interested in school or applying myself. I did not have the kind of role model or mentor in my life that I needed in order to succeed. My home life was very dysfunctional. There was no one to make me do my homework. With all the chaos in the home, I found that my just getting out of the house in the morning in the right frame of mind was an accomplishment in itself. Life in the "hood" seemed to be the survival of the fittest; lots of drama and trauma!

At fifteen or sixteen, I began spending most all of my time hanging out in a local pool hall. Not long afterwards, I was helping one of the partners in the business with his numbers (an illegal gambling racket.) As I got more and more involved in the number rackets, I would always have money in my pocket.

Drugs were sold out of the pool room. I remember when a very famous heavyweight prize fighter's trainer came in and copped some drugs. Go figure! The way the set up was, the owner of the pool hall sold the drugs and I worked for his partner, helping in his number's racket. Oddly enough, both of these guys had a heart of gold toward me and the other kids who hung out there. "I want you guys to stay out of trouble," they'd say, smiling.

In hindsight, it is weird, but even though they were doing the wrong things and I was doing wrong by helping them, it was because of them that I stayed away from the really bad stuff and concentrated on making money. At that time, most of the other young people I'd known since grade school were doing age appropriate things. But I was hanging around guys who could be my father and, in some cases, my grandfather.

Speaking of doing wrong things: I'm aware that a lot of people do some of the things they do out of survival. I was one of them. However, truth be told, this is not right because the means do not justify the end. We can say it's ok to cheat and rob someone because we have to pay the bills or feed our children, but what if it is our loved one who is getting hurt, robbed, taken advantage or killed? I really didn't wholeheartedly learn this lesson until I became a Christian. Prior to this, I was doing my own share of "surviving." When I was younger, it really did not make sense for me to work at a low paying job when I could hustle instead. To me that was stupid. There was a time I would not get caught working in a McDonald's or Burger King. However, today if I really needed to, I would work at not just one low paying job, but two, in order to take care of my family. I would not rob anyone or steal. It's wrong and not a good look for our children. Today, by the grace of God, I know and understand it takes character to make an honest and decent living, as opposed to stealing and robbing.

One day, while playing pool, the wife of the main partner stumbled out of the back of the pool room and fell to the floor. She was foaming at the mouth. Because of my street smarts, I immediately assumed she had overdosed off of drugs. I was right. My friend who had a very sturdy build and was about 6'2 began to slap the lady real hard in an effort to revive her.

I ran to the nearby grocery store to get some milk. I had heard that it helped when someone was overdosing from heroin. I didn't know whether it was true or a myth.

We held her up and gave her the milk. Not long after, the ambulance arrived to take her to the hospital. Later on, I learned that she had died. Her husband was sentenced to several years in the federal penitentiary. There were more than a few shootings in the pool room while I was there.

I learned a few tricks of the trade in the numbers game which caused it to be very lucrative. It happened so many years ago, so I guess I can share it now. The main scheme was that when I would get the call to be told what the winning number would be, I had a way to put in a bet with a fictious name, and then pay myself! It was quite a scam. Even my comrade in arms (Tyrone) didn't know about this. He probably had his own racket. The person responsible to pay off the bets whenever the people picked the winning number was called the banker. Well, there were times that the banker who I worked for suspected that something was out of order. However, he was never able to me catch me red handed.

There was one particular time on my birthday, I was mistakenly given $500 too much money to pay out. In this case, the money had gone through too many hands, so it couldn't be proven that I had the $500. The business had its rewards and its risks. I was robbed three times. Once it was at gunpoint and I was ordered to takeoff my pants and walk for about a block in the snow. When I was seen by my friends who were hanging out on the stoop, they seemed to think it was funny. On another occasion, I was accosted by two masked guys with shotguns who tied up.

In spite of the dangers, I did not quit because of all the money that was involved. I began to ask myself: "Did I really *need* an education? Why take the hard road and do all this work when I could make a lot of easy and not so easy money?" Things finally came to a head one morning while I sat listening to the most boring lecture about hypotenuses something-squared while a student at Charles E. Hughes High School. The negative thoughts really weighed heavily on me like never before. Once again, I said to myself, "Floyd, *what am I doing here?*" For one thing, living in my home & neighborhood—well, it was a different world from this school and these teachers with their rosy outlooks on life. Our tenement building was getting dirtier and more decrepit with every passing year; nothing like this well-lit, freshly-painted school with its shiny polished floors. These teachers were talking about a different world from the one I went back to when I walked out of those doors.

"*What am I doing here?*" That and other new thoughts started occurring. Say I didn't show up in class and the school phoned to check on me. No one was even home now to take the call.

With no adult input to challenge my negative thinking, I began skipping school. Life hanging out on the streets was great. No one bossing me around, and there were opportunities to make money. People there accepted me, so I didn't have to work for the approval that good grades brought. In fact, I didn't have to work at all. I began partying, drinking, smoking reefer, and sniffing cocaine. Who needed some degree—some piece of paper—to get me where I wanted to go? The streets could teach me everything I wanted and needed to know.

In 1975, at the age of eighteen, I was making so much money running the numbers (as they call it) that I officially dropped out of high school. And I became a father. Tianaki was my beautiful baby girl. The only downer was, I was beginning to use drugs more and more. No way was I prepared to give this incredible, gorgeous little girl what she needed and deserved in the way of a stable home. Although I wasn't a heroin addict like my mom and dad, it did cross my mind that I was condemning Tia to the same childhood-minus-a-healthy-daddy I had experienced. I blocked those thoughts out. Instead of choosing the life-road that led through education to a career and stability, I took another road. I'd make my way using my street smarts. It never occurred to for me to ask myself: *"How smart, really, were these choices I was making?"*

5

Angel Dust

Shortly after the birth of my daughter, my hustle in the number's racket was drying up. The guy I worked for lost all of his money and his credibility. To make matters worse, a new drug hit the streets and had taken Harlem by storm. Phenyl cyclohexyl piperidine (PCP), also known as angel dust among other names, is a drug used for its mind-altering effects. PCP can cause hallucinations, distorted perceptions of sounds, and violent behavior. As a recreational drug it is typically smoked, but it may be taken by mouth, snorted, or injected. It may also be mixed with pot or tobacco. Its adverse effects include seizures, comas, addiction, and an increased risk of suicide. Flashbacks may occur even after stopping usage.

When I started smoking angel dust, like most drugs, it was fun at first. I'd laugh, dance, and party with my friends. However, after a while it seemed to be getting out of hand. For one thing, my personality drastically changed. Because of that, my daughter's mother and I broke up. I wasn't *"Floyd, the cool guy with money"* any more. Things didn't work out, and I moved back to my grandmother's tenement building.

It should have dawned on me that my doing angel dust was a *real* problem almost from my first puff. In my head, I thought I'd found heaven. No wonder they call it angel dust. I felt light, strong, and like I could take on the world. I'd never been very athletic, but angel dust gave me amazing strength. Under its influence, I could do a lot of push-ups and sit-ups, and I could ride a bicycle from the very tip of downtown Manhattan to the end of Uptown with no problem.

Yet, there was a downside to my new lifestyle. Once, while on angel dust, I tried to throw a lady friend out the window in Grandma's apartment. The next day I didn't even remember it. And there was the way I was living. Grandma's building had become so gross and run-down that it became condemned. Grandma moved out, and so had the rest of my family—with the exception of me and one cousin, another addict, who was also living in the decrepit apartment. The building that had once housed my family was quickly becoming a haven for druggies and other down-and-outers.

I told myself that I was just temporarily "down on my luck." I refused to face the fact that drug use had made me so unstable that I couldn't even hold down a job. This was a real low point. I had no income. I remember another homeless friend and myself reading the Bible under candlelight, smoking angel dust together! We had no electricity or running water.

While standing out on the stoop one day (in the suburbs they call it the porch), I had this sudden mental picture of myself being stuck in a revolving door going no place; just going in circles. In that moment, I saw three types of people. There were the youth, who were living their lives as such. They were innocent, for now. Then there were the young adults, like myself. For the most part, we were partying and living it up. Some of my friends were getting into trouble with the law and even getting killed. Also, many of them were going into the military. I believe this was being done not so much because they were so patriotic, but because they were wanting to find opportunities outside of Harlem. Lastly, (although everyone does not fit this mold), in the circles that I was in, there were the older people. If they did not work; they pretty much just hung around the neighborhood. It was also common for the men in my community who had jobs to hang out on the corner, drink, chase women, and gamble afterwards.

After getting this vision, I realized that if I didn't make some kind of good move, I was going to be stuck on that revolving door. I also envisioned my beautiful daughter some day in the future coming around the neighborhood in search of me. I could hear her asking for me...and feeling ashamed at the responses. "No, I haven't seen that bum. But if you find him, tell him I want the money I loaned him."

The thought that I would be a disgrace to her cut deeply.

But why couldn't I stop what I was doing? Instead of being heartbroken, I was getting more callused. What was it going to take? My life was becoming a blurred series of ugly snapshots. One day I was smoking-up right on the front stoop of the old tenement and my mind was flying. I just needed to go somewhere, anywhere. Without thinking, I waved down a passing cab. When the driver asked, "Where do you want to go?" I'd said, "Home."

"What's the address?"

I gave it to him and he just looked at me. "You *are* home!"

"Take me *home,*" I shouted, suddenly getting violent.

"Get out of my cab," he roared back.

On another occasion, on my way to buy drugs, I saw a commotion on the sidewalk. Pressing through the crowd, I saw a young guy in a pool of blood. He had gotten shot in the head. It was a drug deal gone bad. I felt no remorse for him. I just stepped around him and went to get my drugs.

On another trip out to get drugs, I passed an alleyway...and smelled an awful, decaying odor. There, sticking out of garbage can was a human body. What did I feel? *Nothing!* However, I became gravely concerned about me...and my state of mind. I knew something was wrong with me. My grandmother didn't raise me to be this way.

50

The so-called proverbial straw that broke the camel's back for me came when I was in an after-hour spot doing cocaine and angel dust. A friend had just lost his mother. "I just want to kill myself," he said over and over. We were doing what we do and all I cared about was that he was messing up my good mood.

"Yo man, don't say that. It's gonna be alright" someone said to him.

Eventually, I left to go up the block. When I came around the corner to the club again, there were cop cars with lights flashing and a crowd. "Someone jumped off the roof," a guy told me. "What a mess!"

The body under the white sheet was my friend. Once again, that's when a voice inside my head said, *"Floyd, you got to make a move. If you don't, you might wind up dead yourself. You were not raised like this. The life you've chosen is insane."*

Back in the dark abandoned building, I felt like I was coming apart. An emptiness opened inside me that was terrifying. I paced back and forth. I swore. I looked at the peeling paint and broken fixtures. Tears swelled, but I was too numb to cry. I felt like I was two steps away from insanity. The way I was living *was* crazy. Taking some black shoe polish, I wrote on the crumbling plaster of a cold wall—*help!*

Psalm 40:1-3 says, *"I waited patiently for the Lord and He heard my cry. He reached down and brought me out of a horrible pit. He set my feet upon a Rock. He established my goings. He put a new song in my mouth. A song of praise.*

God is no respecter of persons. He will answer your prayer, too. He has promised that if you call on Him with a sincere heart, He will come and rescue you.

* * * * *

Somehow, I talked my way into Grandma's new apartment. My cousin had returned to live with her, too. If Grandma had one thing, it was love. But unfortunately it wasn't tough love, which is what I sorely needed. Nina, while trying so hard to help me, actually was hurting me by allowing me to do what I wanted. Allowing me to live with her and live as I pleased was not helpful. Even when I would hold down a job for a while, I would party all weekend long. Coddling me and not holding me accountable caused it to take a lot longer for me to become a man. My grandmother allowed me to do what I did because it eased her anxiety about possibly getting a call on the telephone that something bad had happened to me on the streets. She did deeply love me, and that was about to be sorely tested.

One day, when I knew her church ladies were coming

over for a prayer meeting, I worked her for some cash. As Grandma handed me bills from her purse, she looked me straight in the eyes. "Floyd, don't you use this money to buy that stuff you smoke."

"Okay, Nina," I promised. "I won't."

Down on the street, not twenty minutes later, I got some dust and smoked up. When I walked back in the door, I was high and felt myself climbing higher by the minute. My cousin saw my eyes and said, "Oh no. The church ladies are here. You better not let Nina see you!"

Quietly, I snuck past the living room where the old women sat with open Bibles on their laps. Closing the door to the bedroom, I flopped on the bed. I was soaring now. Then I got up, put an album on and started moving to the beat while looking in the mirror and peeling off my clothes at the same time. I even remember the name of the album! However, I'm not going to give glorify satan. Why should I? He made such a fool out of me.

That was the last thing I remembered until I woke up in bed, seeing Grandma and all the old women standing around me praying. Apparently, I'd walked right into the middle of their prayer meeting without a stitch of clothes on and passed out on the floor. I can't imagine how these old women hauled me to my bed. But I could understand why Grandma looked like she was dying a thousand deaths.

Days and weeks blurred. I was smoking so much dust that strangely I couldn't do reefer any more. So my use of dust picked up a lot. It didn't bother me that under its influence I became irrational. Not long after, the effects of the angel dust caused me to do something crazier than ever. I tracked Grandma down at the apartment of one of her friends who lived just downstairs. Grandma sang in a quartet and had gone there to practice a song for church with three of her friends. Only later would I learn that when the door opened, I staggered inside and crawled into the woman's bed. Raving, out of my mind, I kept calling out to these saintly old ladies to come hop in bed with me and I'd make them glad they did.

When Grandma told me later what I had done, her beautiful old face was lined and drawn with deep, deep soul-sadness. I'd humiliated her in front of her friends. Life seemed to come out of her because of my sinful actions. "I have no happiness in my own home," she said wearily. My grandmother was a trustee as well as one of the mothers of the church. My sinful conduct had made her so sad. How could I go on hurting this dear lady who had loved so much and lost so much? I loved my grandmother dearly and didn't want to be responsible for her death. Had she died while I was in my addiction, I would have felt that I killed her. That would have been unbearable. I could not live with

54

that, yet this is what I was doing. I was sucking the life out of her, little by little.

My grandmother was so special to me that there could have been the argument that when I was in my right mind, she was my "real" girlfriend. She was my heart. I really tried to do right by her even though I was not living right. My love for her would one day cause me to put my hands in my head and cry out to God Almighty to please help me, for I did not want my grandmother to die on my watch.

When I wasn't feeling bad about hurting my grandmother, I also had a good chuckle with my friends about the "old lady incidents." But still, some bad and sobering stuff was going on all around me with people who were taking these strong and dangerous drugs. Under the influence, one girl put her baby in a hot oven and killed her. Another guy jumped off of a bridge. There were people I'd see naked in the streets. The devil was wreaking havoc on the inner city and upon the lives of the countless people who became hooked and seduced by this horrible and powerful drug.

Rap music had caught on and the parties in the hood (to me) were getting wilder. More violent, too. Shootings and fights were a threat at almost any party you went to, so I started avoiding those uptown Harlem scenes in favor of clubs downtown or in the Village where you stood less of a chance of taking a bullet. Basically, all I wanted to do (my priorities) was to get high, party, and be with women. Soon, getting high became my number one, two, and three priorities.

6
Daddy's Home

There was one main influence in my shattered life, an unlikely source of positive inspiration. Right before my drug use really escalated, I had been sitting out on the stoop of the old tenement listening to records with my friends and getting my hair braided. We were all still living in the building then—the entire family except for my sister. From across the street I saw a well-dressed man coming toward me, smiling. He had beautiful, naturally wavy black hair and a nice suit. I was thinking, "Why is this dude smiling at me when he doesn't even know who I..." But as he reached the sidewalk in front me, my jaw dropped. This man was my dad!

Do you remember my dad's friend "Turk" in Chapter One? Turk was the one that gave Dad the skinny about my mother when he was twenty-two years old. She was only fourteen. Well, Turk's real name is Alonzo Smalls. He was the one that God would use to direct my dad to Teen Challenge. Alonzo had become a Christian first through the food program at The Soul Saving Station Church in Harlem. The addicts would come and listen to the Word of God and then they could get something to eat. After Alonzo became a believer, he went to Teen Challenge and then to Bible school. He then returned to help out at The Soul Saving Station. By the grace of God, Alonzo Smalls would become a minister of the gospel and the founding Executive Director of Pivot Ministries located in South Norwalk and Bridgeport, Connecticut. As of the writing of this book, Rev. Alonzo is retired and doing well by the grace God. I've stayed in touch with him, as you can imagine how special he is to me. He is the only person on the planet that I know who knew my mother, and he encouraged my dad to go to Brooklyn Teen Challenge. He's told me some great stories about all of them growing up in Harlem. I even had the privilege of working at his ministry for a season.

My father and I both were soon upstairs, talking to my Aunt Joyce and Grandma. He informed us that he'd become a Christian and had gotten off drugs thanks to help from Teen Challenge. He was also engaged at the time. The lady who would become my step mother was a volunteer at Brooklyn Teen Challenge, where then met. Her name was Barbara, a fine Christian lady; one of the best examples of a Christian lady I have ever known. My dad wanted me to live with him, but although I was very happy for him and I was glad that God gave me my dad back, I chose to stay with my grandmother. My sister Denise did go to live with him and Barbara after they got married.

You know, most of the homes in the inner cities are led by women. Kudos to the black women for the fortitude and success they have had and shown in raising their black children However, mothers cannot be fathers!

I've got to give my dad his props though. Why? Countless families in the inner city are known to be notoriously fatherless and headed by single mothers and grandmothers and the fact that Dad came back for me and my sister I find is awesome. My dad did not have to come back for me, but he did. This is even though I decided not to move to Plainfield, New Jersey with him. My dad could have then settled and been content with his new family. However, he manned up. He did not run away from his responsibilities.

My dad was a quiet man and I always envisioned him as being a man with an iron fist in a velvet glove. To me, he was compassionate and strong. He wasn't perfect, but he was very caring. Up until the day my dad died, he would hug me and kiss me on the cheek. He did this even when I was with my loving and faithful wife (Mary Miles) who I have been married to now for nearly thirty-six years. When he did this, I acted like I did not like it; but I did. It made me feel valued. His affections toward me made up for all of the years that he was not in my life; building up my self-esteem. Even with his being gone now, I can still feel the warmth and security of his embraces.

From then on, Dad tried to see me often. Also, I remember that he used to return to Harlem on the weekends with clothes and Bible tracts to give out to his friends who were still on drugs. He would ask me to go along with him. He kept trying to get me to become a Christian. I kept thinking, "I'm happy for you. You needed Jesus because you were a heroin addict for twenty years. However, I'm not in the kind of shape you were in." Another way of saying this is that there is a so called "pecking order" amongst drug users. What do I mean by this? Well, everybody who smokes pot thinks, *"At least I'm not an alcoholic."* And the alcohol user thinks, *"At least I don't do angel dust.* The "angel dust head" says, *"At least I'm not a low-down heroin addict."*

When I was on the streets, the heroin addict was considered to be the bottom of the barrel. I've never used crack, but I guess the person considered to be at the bottom of the barrel these days on the streets is the crackhead and the meth addict. Regardless of the so-called pecking order, the reality is they are all lost and we all need Jesus. Romans 3:23 says that we all fall short of the glory of God. This even applies to the persons who've never used drugs in their life. They may never have lied, stolen or fornicated. Still, Isaiah 64:4 says, *"Our righteousnesses are as filthy rags."* First John 1:8-9 says, *"If we say we have not sinned, we lie and the truth is not in us. However, if we confess our sins, God is faithful and just to forgive us our sins and to cleanse us from all unrighteousness."*

Dad and my step mon (Barbara) would eventually have children, my brother Johnathon and my sister Sharoya. My sister Denise moved to New Jersey with them, but I stayed in Harlem. Even as my life started to derail, just like Dad's life had, I marveled at the changes in him. He was like a man who'd come back from the dead. Seeing how he was trying to raise his new family made me feel proud of him. He had really changed, and I sincerely wanted to see him continue to succeed.

Occasionally, I'd go visit him in New Jersey and stay a few days. The suburbs were nice, but I was a Harlemite! When I would return from Jersey and arrive at the Port Authority, I'd get on the train and get off at 125th Street and Saint Nicholas Avenue. I would literally look forward to taking a deep breath to take in the foul Harlem air. I loved it!

My dad certainly was no fool, and knew right away that I was on drugs.

"Son," he said, shaking his head, "I know what you're doing. It's no good."

But Dad didn't press. I suppose his strategy was just to befriend me because he didn't want to lose me again. That was smart. If he'd pushed, he would have. As it was, I blew off all Dad's well-intentioned warnings. However, I was never disrespectful to him.

My dad really tried to please me. He actually bought

me two cars. The first one I had for just about two weeks, if that. My friend and I got into an accident on the 135th Street Bridge on the East Side. The second car he got me, the engine seized up.

I sometimes thought back to all the times in the last couple of years my dad had tried to warn me about what I was doing to myself. Once in a while, I'd think, just for a few minutes, *if only I'd listened...*then I'd get high again. Why didn't I have enough sense to spare myself what lay just ahead? I knew that I needed help. It got to the point where I would be asking God to help me at the same time I was getting high. It wasn't fun anymore. Yet, I was still doing it. This is the epitome of addiction!

What followed was a series of peaks and dips. Sometimes I'd manage to pull myself up a little. First, of course, I'd cut back on partying. Just cut back. I'd then get a job. I got my GED and went for some college-level training. During these times, I'd feel like my life was happening again. I even landed really good jobs at great places like the World Trade Center and Chemical Bank.

While working at the World Trade Center, there was a really nice-looking married Christian man named James. The ladies would try to flirt with him, but he was dedicated to his wife and the Lord. He was solely about doing his job and talking about Jesus. I would say to him, "Man, what's wrong with you?" It was funny that even though I was the cool hip guy, I saw something in James' life that I wanted. James was an accomplished gospel singer and some of the executives would invite him to sing at special functions. Strange enough, I even went in the bathroom and while I was in the stall, I wrote "Jesus Saves." Can you imagine that? James went in the bathroom and after he came out, he asked me had I done it? I wanted to lie but I told him the truth.

"Gee!" He said, "That is not the way to do it, Floyd. If you want Jesus Christ in your life, you need to come to church with me." I accepted James' invitation to go with him to his church, which was The Church of Salvation and Deliverance in Harlem. I went there and it was a dynamic and powerful service. I responded to the altar call, but I did not get saved then. However, in hindsight, God was surely working on me.

After getting fired from the World Trade Center job, I soon was working at Chemical Bank. I saw this girl that I liked named Martha, a Christian who attended Brooklyn Tabernacle Church. When I tried to hit on her, she invited me to her church. I said, "Ok." I remember saying to myself, "If that's what I have to do in order to score, so be it." Well, I went to church and Martha was the consummate Christian. She carried herself flawlessly. I would eventually get fired from that job, too because of my poor job performance. I never made it to first base with Martha, either. I didn't even get out of the batter's box. She maintained her testimony. I did not even get a kiss on the cheek. However, her pastor (Jim Cymbala of the Brooklyn Tabernacle) prayed for me and told me that God had a calling on my life. I didn't get saved at that time, either. As a matter of fact, I had to hit rock bottom before I would surrender my life to the Lord.

But just like James, Martha also shared Jesus and her testimony with me. During my lunch breaks on these jobs, even though I was thought to be the hip cool guy in my department, I would go to a nearby empty church and sit quietly, try to meditate, and try to talk to God.

After the "ups" came the "downs." As soon as I felt in control of my life again, I'd slide back into heavy partying. More angel dust went into my lungs and more cocaine went up my nose than I can even remember. Time and time again I'd leave work, grab something to eat, hit a round of parties and wake up the next day around noon, having blown off another morning of work.

It was amazing how much garbage I could come up with to excuse my absence to my bosses. A sudden illness. A family emergency. A dentist's appointment. In the end, my erratic work record and undependable habits always got me fired. I was taking in a lot of drugs. I definitely could not see that each dip was taking me lower and lower. The ride was getting rough again, real fast.

With each passing day, a dull feeling was growing inside me. Not so much a feeling as a sense of emptiness. Outwardly, I was still partying and smiling. But inside, the times of sheer emptiness were scary.

As a matter of fact, I remember being at parties, well-dressed, money in my pocket, a drink in my hand, and a smile on my face. Yet, I was so very lonely. There were times when I just knew there had to be more to life than living for the weekends. It was a ritual! A merry go round! A revolving door! I would get paid, pick up my package, get my clothes out of the cleaners, start getting high little by little before the evening officially started, call the people I was going to hook up with, and then just hit the town!

As I sat in Grandma's house, stoned or depressed, I could see I was worrying her to death. Once, I overheard her praying in her room, fervently crying out to God, "Lord, whatever You do, please do not let my grandson go to Hell. Lord, whatever it takes! If You've got to take an eye…take it! If You've got to take a leg, take it! I'd rather he goes to heaven maimed, than go to Hell whole!" That really woke my conscience. God forbid that she dies with me in this state. I'd carry that guilt for the rest of my life. She prayed that prayer often and hard. A lot of times I would hear her praying so passionately that it would take my high away; and if I ever needed a couple of dollars from her, I would have to wait until after the prayer.

I also discovered that my dad had told her, "Put him out of the house. As long as any of us keeps helping him, he'll never hit bottom and seek the help he really needs." But she had told him, "He's my baby. I can't do that."

It was like my grandmother and dad was playing good cop/bad cop. Of course, she was the good cop. However, one thing for sure is that they wanted the same things for me. Now I was the one on my knees. "God," I begged, "please help me to stop hurting my grandmother." But it was no use. In an hour or so, I was thinking about getting my next high. I did come up with one solution. This would fix everything.

7

My Shattered Dreams

There was this restless dream in me, a hope that literally soared to great heights. I wanted to be in the Air Force. Even though it was competitive, I was sure I could get in. Where the desire came from, I don't know, but I wanted to be an Air Force Chaplain. In any case, things were not working out in the business world for me. Like so many others before me, I saw the military as my ticket out of Harlem and out of the mess my life was in.

Why I wanted to be an Air Force Chaplain is an interesting and strange mystery. Mysteriously, even when I had the devil in me, doing all the wrong things, if I had only taken a good look back, even I could have seen that from day one God had His hand on my life. For instance:

- Church was a very big part of my upbringing.
- I was coming in contact with Christian people such as Martha at Chemical Bank and James at the World Trade Center.
- My love and admiration for Dr. Martin Luther King, Jr. To this very day, he is my most beloved hero. I loved what he stood for, and he was an awesome

preacher.

- Me and my angel-dust-smoking-friend would read the Bible together when we lived in an abandoned building.

- One time, I was with my friends standing on the corner, just wasting time. One of my friends approached us and told us that he had joined a Muslim sect. Then all of us started to talk about what we believed. When it came my turn, with a cigarette in my mouth and a beer can in my hand, I would unashamedly share my belief in Jesus Christ as the Son of God. I pretty much shared the gospel like a seasoned Christian. When I did, the entire corner got quiet. There was a holy hush! Everyone looked at me as if to say, "Where did that come from?" One guy said, "Floyd, what are you doing out here?"

- While doing drugs and ungodly things, I would want to talk about the Bible. Girls that I were with told me that I needed help because I wanted to talk so much about Jesus

- When I was small, my grandmother would dry clean my pastor's robes that he preached in. When she would bring them home, I would put them on, stand in front of the mirror and preach my little heart out.

Yes, without question, in hindsight God had His hand on my life! Honestly, I wanted to go into the armed forces just to get away...to get out of Harlem. There were opportunities for me in Harlem. However, I was on the wrong path.

Then late in the summer of 1980, the Air Force tentatively accepted me. Grandma lost no time bragging to the neighbors. Everyone was thrilled. I was on my way up to a new life! On the September morning I showed up at the enlistment office at Fort Dix in New Jersey, I had my packed bags with me. A few last hurdles, and I'd be on a plane *out of here.* They'd told me I'd fly in San Antonio, Texas. In every sense, I was ready to fly!

Then I stepped on the scales. I'd been warned the Air Force enforced strict weight limits, but I had partied throughout the whole summer. The guy checking me out slid the weights across the scale's balance not once, but twice, then scribbled something on his pad.

"You're over the weight limit, son," the recruiting officer told me. I smiled. "Hey, just give me a couple of hours. I can go out and jog off the water weight." But it was a no-go. "You were given the weight limits when you signed up," he said flatly. "The Air Force expects you to take it seriously. Apparently, you didn't. Sorry, but there are no exceptions."

They offered me another ship-out date a few months later. But I was devastated. All the way back to Harlem I cried like a baby. I'd thought I was escaping this place and my miserable life, but it had pulled me right back. In my mind's eye I pictured myself as a guy who was reaching for a high goal...but I didn't have what it took...and it slipped out of my grasp. It couldn't have been worse if they'd taken a rubber stamp and stamped my forehead with the word "Rejected." I was going home in humiliation and defeat.

I will never forget when my grandmother came home and saw me there. Once again, I literally saw life come out of her. She was so disappointed. Nothing that I told her mattered. She didn't even believe me. She thought that I had ran some type of scam.

Now the ground fell out from under me inside. The only things I'd ever had to hold on to all my life were *outside* me. Money, drugs, friends, the party-guy image. *Inside* there was nothing. Dreams blew away, and every day I plunged further into a pit of emptiness.

Within a month, my whole personality changed. Disappointment turned into depression. All I knew to do to get out of my sorry self was to throw myself deeper into drugs. It was a quick slide down. *Numb* is the only word to use for where I lived in the coming weeks. Numb from cold. Numb from the inside. Numb as snapshots of reality blurred together with my angel dust and cocaine highs.

Instead of focusing on meeting the requirements to get into the Air Force, things for me got much worse. One night I found myself amongst total strangers standing around a burning garbage can to stay warm. I remember my gazing into the fire, taking swigs of black berry brandy, thinking about my life. The black berry brandy was to help me to stay warm.

However, the reality is that when it comes to alcohol consumption, during the digestion process, the liver gives off heat as it metabolizes the alcohol. Therefore, it creates a feeling of being warm, but is in fact lowering a person's core body temperature. Though a person may sweat, their temperature is not actually rising, but lowering.

God has perfect timing, though! Hallelujah! Finally, all the things my dad had been telling me over the years started making sense to me. And he was the one person on Earth I believed I could turn to. I knew it would not matter to my dad what I was doing. His love was free, without condition or reserve. So I contacted him and he came right away.

"I'm not perfect, son," my dad said. "Far from it as a matter of fact. But you know and have seen what God did for me, son. The Lord helped get me off drugs."

As my dad talked, something happened inside me. I saw Dad talking to me the way a loving father *should* talk to his son. And I felt all the lost years when drug use had kept us from having this type of relationship. And more than that, I saw my beautiful little Tia. Five years old now. I saw that I'd fallen into the same lifestyle and repeated the vicious cycle—subjecting her to the same abandonment and neglect I suffered. I broke inside. No way was I going to put my little daughter through that kind of degrading humiliation any more.

Desperate as I was, willing as I was to change, I still had serious doubts. Even with Dad—a living miracle—sitting right there in front of me, handing me tissues to wipe my eyes, I didn't really believe that *I* could ever change. Harlem had been my family. My life. Harlem *had* me and I didn't think I could ever escape.

"Just this once, son," my father said as I folded my arms in front of me in unbelief, "don't try to go it alone. You've always had to make your way alone. You've had to be self-sufficient; do it all on your own. If you can find it in yourself, I'm asking you, son, open up just this one time. Let someone get inside to help you. Reach out to something and Someone beyond yourself. Go to the program in Brooklyn where I found the help I needed…and you will too!

I slowly opened my arms and my hands went limp to my tired sides. Dad reached out his right hand, and I reached up and shook his waiting hand and said, "Ok. Ok, I'll go."

8

From Doubt...To Dawn

When I walked through the doors of the Teen Challenge Center in Brooklyn, it was a cold February morning in 1982. I had some hope, but also some serious doubts. This was the same Center my first cousin and my dad had gone to, years before. These people, whoever they were, had helped to bring about a major change in a man who'd been a hopeless heroin addict for *nineteen years.*

My first cousin Rennie was three years older than me. On the streets, he was into some things that I wasn't. He was at another level! Also, it didn't help that I was mistaken for him, at times. While in the program, his life also changed dramatically. As a matter of fact, he would return home and witness to me. One time he was ministering with the Teen Challenge Choir at the well-known Soul Saving Station Church, located in Harlem. When I entered the church and saw my cousin ministering on the stage, I saw that his face shined like Moses in the Bible. The presence of God was so powerful in the service that I had to immediately sit down. I'd never experienced anything like that before.

For the first two weeks I was at Teen Challenge, I felt

73

a stirring of something new and different inside. Mixed in with the doubt was a small bit of *happiness and relief.* An opportunity opened up for me to go to the Brooklyn Teen Challenge Camp Champion in Upstate New York.

Man...when I arrived there, I was not disappointed! Here I was straight out Harlem, and now living on the beautiful campground in this pristine environment. I was so relaxed and at peace. I remember telling one guy who was acting like he was still in the city that he didn't have to do that here. There was no need to wear masks and try to be someone that you're not.

The surroundings were so beautiful that I would even feel guilty for being there. Why did I feel this way? Because I knew that I had left some good people behind. Contrary to what a lot of people think, there are some good people in the inner city who use drugs. There is no need to fear everyone in the inner city. I even cried because while I was enjoyed the three hots and a cot on that beautiful campground, I knew what some of my friends would be doing at certain times of the day and night. It made me sad because I wanted them to get the break that I got, too. A load of guilt came down on me because of that. I was getting a break. A lot of friends weren't getting this same chance. Every morning as I woke to the quiet sound of a fresh breeze and birds singing, I could picture the friends who were no doubt smoking-up in a hallway of a tenement building somewhere in Harlem. My own mom had died of heroin—she never got her break.

Along with those doubts was the big question. I'd been on drugs so long; would I make it? I still remember the day the change began inside me; the day when my doubts about making it began to clear, replaced by the first lights of a new dawn inside me. It was only a stray remark by a counselor in the midst of a longer talk—but it exploded inside me: "People who are hooked on drugs or alcohol tend to see things only from a self-centered point of view. They tend to see all the bad things life handed them; everything that was denied them. Sure, a lot of us had really, really bad things happen to us. But we also tend to overlook all the good things that God and other people did for us every single day."

In my mind's eye there was Grandma: struggling, working hard to support us all against the toughest odds. I'd always thought about how lousy it was to lose my mother and have no father around. There was Grandma and my aunt, loving, sacrificing their whole lives for me and the others. And I'd stolen from Grandma, used her, lied to her…and there were Grandma's friends at the Mt. Moriah Baptist church who had fervently prayed for me for years. Something was stinging my eyes as the counselor went on talking…

And there was a guy named James at the World Trade Center. He was as sold out to God as anyone I'd ever met. He'd befriended me, told me about God's love, taken me to church so I could turn my life around. And there was Martha, a co-worker I'd hit on at Chemical Bank. She resisted those efforts because she was a Christian, but had cared about me and prayed for me, nonetheless. It hit me. Through these people and others who flooded my memory, God had been trying to love me and reach to me for many years. I had been too self-centered to even see it.

Thanks to the godly people at Teen Challenge, I was being given the right perspective to look at my life. That was the moment doubt began to go and a new light began to dawn. In that quiet moment, I bowed my head and prayed—surrendering my life, finally, to God...to my Lord, Jesus Christ. Afterwards, I remember feeling clean and brand new. 2 Corinthians 5:17 says, *"Therefore, if any person be in Christ, he is a new creation. Old things have passed away and all things have become new."*

The thing I learned very quickly about drug addicts was this: while we were on drugs, pretty much all our interior growth *stopped.* When you're that focused on yourself...and only on getting the next hit...and on using other people and their money for your own ends, you don't have time for the healthy maturity that comes from getting involved in good relationships with other people; the kind where you learn to share life by learning to give as well as take.

This is where Teen Challenge did some very important things for me. First, it gave me the chance to literally get out of my old setting. That alone cleared my head. But along with that, these good people challenged me to take a look at my life from the outside. *How did I relate to people? Did I use people? What did I really do that was of any use or value to other people?*

My main answer to these questions really *stung— mostly I was focused on myself and my own good time. I hadn't cared about Grandma. Not even myself, really.*

What I felt was a good sting—like putting medicine on a nasty, infected sore. What made it bearable was that, along with the challenge, the Teen Challenge people assured us over and over that God is quick to show mercy and forgiveness when we're finally honest about our lives and ourselves. As I stopped excusing my misuse of other people, I could feel my soul healing more every day; becoming alive and human again.

There were so many other things I got from my time at Teen Challenge. Besides the spiritual guidance and drug counseling, there was something else about these people I couldn't quite put my finger on. Once, on a weekend's pass home, I fell right back into drug use. When I left to go home on my pass, I really had no intention of getting high. I was a stellar student. I had asked Jesus into my heart and had fully bought into what I was being taught. When I was in Teen Challenge, I used to walk around like I was in college. I had gotten baptized again because now it meant more than just being cute. I was serious and trying to apply what they were teaching me.

Prior to my going home, I saw that all the other guys were staying inside during their pass. The reason they did this was because they were afraid that they would fall. I would joke and say, "Y'all stayed home and watched the soap operas like little girls." I thought they were weak! I remember saying, "Y'all...I'm saved, sanctified, and filled with the Holy Ghost. Why would I have to stay in the house on my pass?"

Well...when I went home, it was Harlem week. Normally, this would have been a great time for me. There were not too many things that made me feel more proud of being an Afro American than this annual event. The atmosphere was electric and festive. Throngs of people lined Seventh Avenue. It was as if the entire community from 110th Street to all the way Uptown was partying. Bands from all over the nation converged on Harlem. The climax was the historically black College Grambling and Morgan State Marching Band heading towards Yankee Stadium to play. Growing up, given that our apartment was on Seventh

Avenue, there was no better view that anyone could have.

I was cool for a while. I should have known that I was going to be tested and have a rough weekend when a young lady who I had not seen for a while greeted me with a kiss on the cheek and told me that I looked good. My response was that I had been upstate chilling out. I didn't mention anything about Jesus. Immediately, I knew that I had sold Him out and threw Him under the proverbial bus. I remember feeling like Judas in the Bible who betrayed Jesus for 30 pieces of silver. What had convicted me so bad was the Scripture found in Luke 9:26— *"If anyone is ashamed of Me and My words, then the Son of Man will be ashamed of you when He comes in his glory."*

I continued on to my grandmother's house where I laid on the bed and told the Lord that I was sorry. However, even after that, I justified going around the block where I used to buy drugs to see if I would run into some people I knew. I would wind up using drugs. I bought some angel dust. The funny thing is that I did not get high, but I did fall into the temptation. I failed the test. Instead of going home, I ran over to see one of the pastors from my home church, Mt. Moriah Baptist Church. Pastor Bailey and his wife were friends of my grandmother.

When I told him what I did, I was very remorseful. I was crying frantically and mucus was coming out of my nose. I got down on my knees and he prayed for me and called my grandmother. Needless to say, I stayed in the house until I had to return to Camp Champion.

I learned some valuable lessons. It is not a sign of weakness to be still if and when you feel that you are not strong enough for a situation and can't handle it. Proverb 16:18 says that pride goes before a fall. I had been too confident! I learned that those guys who were staying in the house at that time when they returned home on their passes were not sissies. They were using wisdom.

When I returned to Camp Champion, I thought they might give up on me. Maybe even kick me out of the program.

"Actually," the counselors told me, "Floyd, *we* knew where you were in terms of kicking this stuff. But *you* needed to know where you were." I could hardly believe the insight, wisdom, love and compassion—not to mention the grace they used in handling me.

I had been in the program for two months when the Director invited us all over one evening. There under their Christmas tree was a nicely wrapped gift box for me. I tore the paper off my package and inside was an expensive sweater. My mouth fell open.

That's when I recognized what it was about these people who were helping to change my life. It was *love.*

Along with everything else I was receiving at Teen Challenge, I was loved.

Although, all of this took place so many years ago, it was just in recent years that I picked up the phone, called Don Wilkerson (Co-Founder of Teen Challenge and Times Square Church) and confessed that I looked into his medicine cabinet when he invited all of us to his house during that holiday season. Of course, nothing was in it. Don was street savvy himself and too smart to do a fool thing like leave meds in his bathroom cabinet while the TC guys were over. In my defense, I told him that I was only in the program for a short while. We got a good laugh out of me sharing this.

To this day, more than thirty plus years later, I am thankful that God loved me enough to deliver me from drug addiction. His power—the healing power of love—reached out and gave another chance to a kid who began life without much of a chance. I'm thankful, too, that He opened my eyes so that I could see His love coming to me (regardless of race) through the men and women of Teen Challenge. To God, and to them, I am eternally grateful.

9

Lessons on the Way to San Antonio

By the grace of God I was saved in 1981, almost forty years ago! And I finally made it to San Antonio, the very same place I had hoped to do my Air Force Boot Camp training so long ago. I had been rejected at Fort Dix in New Jersey because of my weight. Actually, my goal was to still go into the Air Force after I completed Teen Challenge. However, God had different plans for me.

While in the Teen Challenge program at a worship service in Upstate New York, I responded to an altar call and the man of God told me exactly what I was thinking. God supernaturally gave Evangelist Morris Cerullo a Word of Knowledge about me. Mr. Cerullo pointed me out and literally told me what I was thinking. Martin Luther King, Jr., one of my heroes whom I have always looked up to, was in my thoughts that evening. Specifically, in the service I was debating in my mind if I should continue to pursue my goal to go into the Air Force, or if I should instead go into the ministry. No one knew it but God, but I had this dream to be like Dr. King, Jr., a minister of the Gospel whom I admired so much. Morris Cerullo said (under the unction of the Holy Spirt), *"You are debating whether you are to go into the Armed Forces or into the ministry. God has called you into the ministry."* That confirmed to me that I was to go to Bible school instead of the Armed Forces.

After I graduated from Teen Challenge, I attended a Bible Institute in Sunbury, Pennsylvania where I met my lovely wife, Mary. To date, we have been married for nearly thirty-six years and have four children (Tia, Jeana, Floyd IV and Tyler) and five grandchildren (Cassidy, Cody, Nylah, Kamani and Kenzi).

After Bible Institute, I received a Bachelor of Science degree from New Hampshire College. From there, I enrolled at Gordon Conwell Theological Seminary in South Hamilton, Massachusetts where I received a Master's Degree in Religious Education. I was ordained with the Assemblies of God in 1992. By God's grace, in addition to serving on a number of boards and committees and being a licensed chemical dependency counselor, I served at Teen Challenge New England for nearly twenty years. While serving there, I was appointed by the Southern New England District of the Assemblies of God to pioneer the first Teen Challenge Center in the state of Connecticut.

I was fortunate to later serve as the lead pastor at Victory Christian Center Assembly of God, located in Indianapolis, Indiana. It was an inner-city church that I faithfully served for nearly eight years as a bi-vocational pastor. No matter how busy I was then, I took vacations with my family, determined to not allow the ministry to dominate and overtake our personal home life. An older minister had wisely warned me of the dangers of putting the ministry before my wife and children.

Since arriving in San Antonio, Texas, I've had the privilege and honor to serve as the Executive Director of the Adult & Teen Challenge of Texas, San Antonio Men's Campus and the ATCOT's Director of Operations. Currently, I serve in the corporate office as the Director of Training. Before ending my story, I want to share a few of the many helpful lessons I have learned on my long journey, written in somewhat chronological order.

Lesson One: The Baptism of the Holy Spirit is for you!

According to the book of Acts, the baptism in the Holy Spirit with the initial evidence of speaking in tongues is available to all believers. The reason why God baptizes His children in the Holy Spirit is to endue us with power to serve and to be effective witnesses. Experiencing it gives the believer extra power from God to serve Him, live for Him, be a witness, and be more effective in sharing His message.

This blessing comes after salvation. This means that

I was a Christian before receiving the baptism of the Holy Spirit. However, once again, this gift from God is available to all who ask for it. I was baptized in the Holy Spirit with the evidence of speaking in tongues when I was in Bible School. I'm still a work in progress. However, my receiving the baptism in the Holy Ghost definitely had a positive effect on my life just like it did for those in the early church. Romans 1:16 says, *"I am not ashamed of the gospel of Jesus Christ for it is the power of God unto salvation."* To me, this Scripture best describes the effect of my receiving the baptism. It gave me power, boldness, and confidence to serve God better and to be a better witness for Him.

Lesson Two: Mercy is stronger than punishment.

Once, while I was a student in the program, I deserved to be punished when I was caught mopping the floor with a dirty mop. Instead of disciplining me, my counselor put his arm around me and quietly said, "Floyd, you can do better than that." I was being lazy and got busted. When he told me, my eyes watered up with repentant tears.

Today, no one can sweep and mop a room better than me because of that example. Mercy *is* stronger than punishment.

Lesson Three: Doing what's right
in God's eyes may seem crazy to others.

While working at the World Trade Center before I was a believer, I submitted a false report to workman's comp. The previous night I had a fight Uptown in Harlem over some money that was owed to me and I fell and hurt my shoulder. I told my employers that I had fallen down the work escalator. I would eventually get fired from there, but the claim was still valid.

The case was finally decided and I was to receive $25,000. By that time I was in Teen Challenge and had invited Jesus into my heart. I told my counselor about it and decided not to take the money. I remember a lot of people telling me that I was crazy. Doing what's right in God's eyes may seem crazy to others, but a clean conscience is priceless!

Lesson Four: Being our brother's keeper may require
holding them accountable if we really care for them.

While a student in Teen Challenge, because I wanted to excel, I used to tell the guys that if they were going to do something bad, not to do it around me because I was telling. It didn't make sense to me to spend an entire year in a Christian program acting the same way that I acted on the streets. I wanted no part of that. Genuine friends who really cared for one another and wanted the best for each other would not do that, I don't think.

WARNING: What I'm about to talk about now is going to get a lot of flak from the "homies/street folk," but I'll say it anyway. There is the saying, *"Snitches get stitches."* That saying is true on the streets and it's the code of conduct in jail, no doubt! However, it's not in the Bible. The Bible says in Proverbs 27:5, 7, *"Open rebuke is better than secret love. The kisses of an enemy may be profuse, but faithful are the wounds of a friend."* This means that I love you enough to challenge you and hold you accountable. That is, of course, if we are really friends. Genesis 4 teaches us that we are our brother's keeper, and that may require telling on them. I don't particularly like people who claim to care a great deal about me and have my back, giving me dabs and high five's. Yet, at the same time, they are not helping me, not looking out for my best interests and are actually trying to lead me down the wrong road. I can do bad by myself.

Lesson Five: God is still in the miracle-working business!

One of the blessings of being part of a faith-based ministry like Adult & Teen Challenge these many years (as a student, staff member, director, and now a corporate officer) is witnessing God's miracle-working power on a daily basis. I could give you a thousand examples to verify that God is still in the miracle-working business today, but I will pick just one; a humorous one.

Once there was a student who was in the program who could not read. Everyone knew that he could not read at all. He never had. However, one day, he was in the dining hall and he just started screaming out, "Hey everybody, I can read! I can read!" The student had randomly picked up a Bible and started reading it out loud. He said, "Look y'all," and he started reading words. It was truly a miracle. No one had taught him. Yes, God is still in the miracle-working business!

Lesson Six: We ALL are in need of a Savior.

When I would travel with the young men into churches to preach and present the Teen Challenge ministry, I did it in a way as if we were the bad guys and the people we were talking to were the good guys. Then God made it clear to me that all of us fall short. Everybody needs Jesus. Romans 3:23 tells us that everyone has sinned. We all fall short of God's glory. If you have never used drugs, you're still a sinner in need of Jesus. Your sins are just different than an addict's.

If you're proud of the fact that you don't have issues

like addicts do, your issue is thinking you don't have any issues! We all do. John 3:16-19 says, *"For God so loved the world that He gave His only begotten Son, that whoever believes in Him should not perish but have everlasting life. For God did not send His Son into the world to condemn the world, but that the world through Him might be saved. He who believes in Him is not condemned; but he who does not believe is condemned already, because he has not believed in the name of the only begotten Son of God. And this is the condemnation, that the light has come into the world, and men loved darkness rather than light, because their deeds were evil."*

Lesson Seven: God may not come when you want Him to, but He's always on time.

I was serving on the Board of Directors of the former Zion Bible Institute (now North Point Bible College), a Pentecostal A/G Bible school. David Wilkerson, the founder of Teen Challenge, was the speaker for the graduation that evening. I was sitting on the rostrum. One thing I remember that he (Dave Wilkerson) did was to ask the audience to stop clapping and commenting while he was preaching. He told the audience that the Holy Spirit didn't need any help. Ouch!

During that particular service, I was serving at the

Teen Challenge Center in Brockton. For some reason, on that night I wasn't feeling very well. My mood was not the greatest. To be honest, I was trying to push through some things.

After Brother Dave's sermon, I was out and about, praying for the graduates. There happened to be a fellow graduating that I knew. He saw me and came over to talk to me. He was very upbeat, jovial, and grateful for all God had done in his life. He was very talkative, too. Little did he know that at the time I had very little interest in all he was sharing with me. That was until I realized that what he was telling me was that, by the grace of God, it was my prayers and pouring into his life that led him to Bible school. He said that had I never encouraged him, he would not have gone. He even remembered the exact message I had preached when he was in the program when he accepted Jesus into his life. It was the story of Naaman when he caught leprosy in II Kings, Chapter 5.

Also, this young man told me that I had prayed for him to get married when he was in the program and that now he was happily married with a family. Long story short: God used this gentleman's testimony to encourage me. Needless to say, my spirit was revived after listening to him. I had overcome what was bothering me. God had sent this gentleman my way just in the nick of time. Since then, there have been countless times when God has showed up right when I needed Him! What's that saying? *God may not come when you want Him to, but He's always on time!*

Lesson Eight: It's not about the money.

One of the students in a bout of being disrespectful towards me said, *"Rev. Miles, why don't you go outside and get a real job!"* I didn't get upset. I waited a few seconds and very graciously responded back to him: *"A baseball player likes to hit home runs. Basketball players like to slam dunk. Football players like to make touchdowns, and I simply like to see people's lives changed by the power of God. It's not about the money. And young man...God will change your life, if you allow Him to."*

Lesson Nine: If you want to live long, honor your parents and grandparents!

When I surprised my girlfriend Mary with an engagement ring, she said yes, but her mom was not too happy because she wanted Mary to finish Bible school first. So Mary and I waited. I was engaged to her for three long years. God honored and blessed the fact that we waited. We celebrated our 35th wedding anniversary in August of 2020.

After I graduated Brooklyn Teen Challenge, I was welcome to return to Harlem to live with my grandmother. I had my head on straight and was doing the right things. However, I said that instead of doing that, I was going to try to make a man of myself and have a place where my grandmother could one day come and relax. Nearly fifteen years later, Mary and I had bought our first home in Connecticut and my grandmother came to visit.

One afternoon she caught me staring at her and asked me what I was thinking? She was lying on the couch in the living room, watching TV. I came in the room, sat down, and told her that story of how, after I graduated from Teen Challenge, I vowed that I would try to get a place that she could come. When I looked at my grandmother laying on the couch, the Lord had told me that day was the fulfillment of my vision and pledge. My Nina had lived to see me turn my life around and she came and relaxed in our home. It wasn't too long after that that my grandma took ill and the Lord called her home. As a matter of fact, when we gathered for prayer before her trip back to Harlem, she stopped me right in the middle of praying when I asked the Lord to keep her safe until she returned the following year. She did this because she was telling us that she was preparing to go and be with Jesus and that she would not be returning. My grandmother was my rock. She had always said things to me that made me feel valued.

Ephesians 6:2-3 says, *"Honor your father and mother, which is the first commandment with promise: that it may be well with you and you may live long on the earth."*

Lesson Ten: The hood and the burbs
are two different worlds.

The late Bishop Raul Gonzalez was a graduate of Teen Challenge, senior pastor of Glory Chapel International Cathedral, and founder of Youth Challenge International (a ministry similar to Teen Challenge). I met him while I was in the program. He literally came through one day, hollering my name, but I didn't know him from Adam! However, what I learned was that he saw my name on the Dean's List when he visited Camp Champion. When Brother Raul saw me and I told him who I was, he told me that when he saw my name posted on the list, he thought it was my father. They knew each other. From that day on, I developed a close relationship with Rev. Raul. He came to the Bible school I attended to speak and would give me a lot of good advice.

One thing that he said to me that I never forgot was, "Floyd, there is a different gospel for the hood than for the suburbs." I understand that hearing this out of context may sound like heresy. However, he was simply saying that different challenges are presented and faced while ministering in the inner city. Sin is sin, but the inner city has a unique culture of its own. He said, "You've got to flow a little differently in the hood," and he's right.

My wife saw a little of this in me when we would visit New York City. One time she said, "Floyd, who are you?" What she meant by that is that when we went to the city, she saw a vivid change in my personality; how I talked and acted. I told her that you have to have "swag" in the city.

My wife had a habit of pulling out all of her money when she went to buy something. I told her not to do that in the city. Also, she would stare at people. That was a no no, too. They would ask you if there was a problem and cuss you out. When I'd ask someone for directions, she said that I talked differently. I told her, "Yeah, that's right. I could come off like I was a square and didn't know my way around the city and I might get jacked!" (robbed) The hood and the burbs surely are two different worlds.

In the next chapter, I humbly submit some personal lessons I have learned regarding racism.

10

Personal Lessons Regarding Racism

As mentioned in Chapter Three, our country was in turmoil during my time growing up in the sixties. Black people were in an uproar because we simply and desperately wanted equality, justice, and freedom. I'm certainly no expert, but if you'd allow me, I'd like to share some thoughts and experiences of my personal struggles regarding racism in the church and in the world today.

Regarding Malcolm X (the controversial Civil Rights Leader): one day while visiting my mother's, granddad's and aunt's graves, I saw a red, black and green American flag on the ground on a nearby grave. It was only about five graves away from where I was standing. Because I was curious, I walked over to that grave. The headstone read, "El Malik Shabazz." I knew that was Malcolm X's name, but I didn't think he would be buried in a common grave. I saw one of the grounds keepers and asked him about it, and he confirmed that it really was Malcom X's grave. Wow! Now I had a dilemma. I had purchased some flowers to put on my family's graves, and I thought to take some of the flowers and put them on Malcolm X's grave. However, this became a dilemma for me to do because of my Christian faith and beliefs. What was causing me to hesitate in putting the flowers on the grave of Malcom X was the fact that he was a Muslim. The Bible says that if he died in his sin without knowing Jesus as his personal Savior, he would not be in heaven. I believe the Word of God! I thought that it would be inappropriate as a Christian minister to put flowers on his grave. Yeah...I was really tripping out. And all the while I was taping all of this on video, because when it was confirmed to me that the gravesite did really belong to Malcom X, I got my huge camcorder out of the car. I put it on top of my car and started recording my private ceremony. I wanted to show everybody I knew that I really was at the grave site of the famous Malcolm X.

Well, I decided to pray and ask for God's guidance and wisdom in regards to whether I was to put flowers on Malcolm's grave. Here is where I came out: I decided that where Malcolm X is spending eternity is between him and God, and none of my business. All that I knew for sure was that Malcom X (a Muslim) loved and stood up for black people. He did this when even some Christians did not. Malcolm X did soften some of his views prior to his death. He and Martin Luther King, Jr. were eventually able to see many things eye to eye. I split the flowers that I had and proudly put some of them on Malcolm's grave. I thought it was a very good decision. I don't often get back to visit my mom's gravesite at the Ferncliff Cemetery in Hartsdale, NY (about 25 miles from Harlem). However, whenever I do, I always put flowers on my family's grave and Malcom X's grave.

Recently, a young Caucasian gentleman I knew was taking some remedial courses in a Bible college. He showed me *The Autobiography of Malcolm X* that was assigned to read. I said to him, "What on earth are you doing with that?" He said that it was required reading to show students how an uneducated person can become very bright from reading. That was Malcolm X's testimony. He read profusely in prison. I smiled at the young man because I found it fascinating that a traditional Bible school would use that particular book. I remember saying to myself, "At least those young people are getting to know about Malcolm X." For years, his autobiography had been banned from many schools.

Also, recently, when George Floyd was needlessly murdered on national TV by a deranged police officer, I was invited to be on a panel to discuss possible solutions to end racism, and how to ease the tension that our nation was experiencing during that time. Unfortunately, these kinds of tragedies have happened much too often over the years. Every time it does, it seems I am asked to share what I think. I'm honored to do so because I get the opportunity to represent Jesus and present His teachings as real and appropriate solutions. Like Dr. King, I "still" believe that sharing and demonstrating God's love and applying the principles in the Word of God are solutions to our society's ills. Yes, it is complicated. For example, this problem is not in every city, and all law enforcement people are not bad people. The issue is not black and white. (No pun intended!) 1 Peter 4:8 says, *"Hatred stirs up strife, but love covers a multitude of sins."*

Also, every time something like this happens, it seems (in my circles) that only the grassroot people and those experiencing the victimization and prejudice are asked to be a part of the panel discussions. The powerful people who have the authority and wherewithal to "really" change things are never present. To me, the organizers are asking the wrong people to be a part of the panel and the panel moderators are asking the wrong people the questions. As I sat on a recent discussion panel, I remember asking, "Why am I here? I didn't do anything wrong."

If we go back to the issue that Rev. Don Wilkerson raised (in the forward on page seven), ironically, my dad said the same thing nearly fifty years ago in the last chapter of his autobiography, *Black Tracks*. The point that I am trying to make is that neither me or my dad or this book can change things. God (of course) along with people in positions to make real changes are the solutions. *"Faith without works is dead"* (James 2:26).

An important note—the goal of this book is to share my personal journey, so far. God is not through with me yet. However, I did feel the need to briefly address the issue that Rev. Don has raised.

I'm extremely grateful for all the civil rights activists. I recognize that today I'm standing on their proverbial shoulders. Also, this applies to the black Assembly of God ministers who went before me and even some who are my contemporaries: Rev. Spencer Jones, Rev. Zollie Smith, Rev. Michael Nelson, Rev. Malcolm Burleigh, Rev. Bob Harrison and Rev. John Aniemeke. Other black clergy who I respect and have inspired me and/or poured into my life are Rev. Ezra Williams, Rev. Alonzo Small, Bishop William Seymour, Bishop Charles Blake, Rev. Norman Miller, Bishop TD Jakes, Dr. Tony Evans and Rev. Earl Johnson.

I have many Caucasian and non-black ministers whom I consider my spiritual dads and I am indebted to, as well: Dave and Don Wilkerson; John Q. Kenzy, Rev. Otis Stanley, Rev. Robert Wise; Rev. Bob Buescher, Rev. Otis Stanley, and Rev. Joe Paskewich. People need to understand that there were white people and people of all races (just like today) who took a stand for equality and justice for black people. Red, Yellow, Black or White...we're all precious in His sight!

Racism is very real and it is very evil. However, some of my issues with race I realize have been *my issues.* I do not wish to blame anyone else for them. For instance, I left my very first sectional meeting as a licensed A/G minister in 1987. This is because I felt like I did not fit in. I remember leaving and calling my wife (on a public telephone). It was raining and I was emotional. I explained to her that I was the only black guy there and it felt like oil and vinegar. The two don't mix. However, in hindsight I feel that I have to own that behavior. That was more my baggage and my issue. Why? Because, even though I didn't know anyone there, which was awkward and could easily bring about anxiety, no one there called me out, was unfriendly, or anything like that. So, I was the only black man there. It didn't seem to bother anyone else, so why should it bother me?

There was another time when I visited a church as a Teen Challenge representative. It was a banquet. However, instead of joining the fellowship, I gave my tickets away and stayed in the sanctuary upstairs, feeling lonely and out of place because I was the only black person there. However, once again in hindsight, I'm owning these feelings and behavior. Why? Because when this happened, I was more seasoned and experienced. By that time, I had lots of genuine friends of all races and colors. As a matter of fact, many of them were inviting me to come and join everyone downstairs, but I allowed that gloomy spirit to stay on me.

Thank God, I'm not like that today. I have much more confidence. (Actually, Holy Ghost SWAG!) I can walk into any place now and know how to handle myself. However, in no way am I an extrovert. Unlike some people who get their strength and energy from being with people, I get my strength from my alone time. My alone time gives me the grace and strength to be social. I prefer it like this. Today, I can be comfortable in my own skin, even if I am the only black in the room and...even if I get vibes that I'm not liked or welcomed. This is because of what God and the Bible has taught me over the years; things like: *"I am fearfully and wonderfully made"* (Psalm 139:14). God's Word also says that I was created in His image and that He loves me unconditionally. He loved me in the Book of Genesis when He created us...just because. I did not have to do anything to earn His love and acceptance when I was born. And...He loves me no matter what.

My logic because of this is: If I don't have to do flips for God to accept me, I'm not going to do them for any other person to accept me. If, for any reason, someone feels a certain way about me just because I'm black and (let's say) they don't like the way I look (my lips or hair, etc.), well, that is their problem, and not mine. My features are just different. Nothing is wrong with them! I'm not bothered by that anymore. As I said, God loves me and I am unique. I heard TD Jakes once say that, *"No one can be me better than me."* Hearing that literally changed my life.

For example, when I first started out in ministry it was very common for me to present TC to politicians, business people, and civic leaders. I used to be petrified to talk if I was the only black person at the table. I dreaded to be asked to say something. When I did, I felt like I would stumble over my words. But that was not the fact. That was a lie. I'm not stupid. I am smart. I learned that what I bring to the table can't be duplicated by anyone else. It is my perspective. I can't be another person or bring what they bring to the table. They have their own experiences, journey, and perspective, and I have mine. Just because mine is different does not make it inferior in any way. I now celebrate who I am, my experiences, my journey, my perspective, etc.

My goal to be an executive director and not settle for mid-level leadership was really an aggressive vision to have because there were no executive directors like me at the time. That bothered me. It might be different now, but when I served in New England you could count the number of Assembly of God churches with an Afro American lead pastor from New York to Maine on one hand. You might have some fingers left over. That deeply bothered me.

Over all, for the most part, I experienced nothing but pure unadulterated godly love. Even today, I have very close friends who I'm still in contact with. However, there were a few times when I was not recognized as the lead representative of Teen Challenge when we arrived at a church. I wouldn't preach and sometimes the pastor would speak for me instead of carting me out to talk to the congregation. This was the exception and not the rule and the churches are not A/G all of the time.

A seasoned leader once asked me in front of some people why did Afro Americans think so highly of MLK, Jr. Although stunned, I did not get upset or act out of character. I chose not to lecture him about the details of the Civil Rights Movement, but on the trip to the conference with the group, we had to stop for food and to relieve ourselves. I told him that had it not been for Dr. King and others, I would have had to use a different bathroom when we stopped, and that my white friend and brother would have had to bring my food out to me and we'd all eat in the van because I would not have been allowed to enter the restaurant. After I said that, the leader grinned and patted me on the back. He said, "Floyd, that is why we need guys like you."

In my early years of ministry, the issues of race and what I thought I was witnessing was quietly having a negative effect on my health. How could that be? I'm from Harlem. It's not possible to be blacker than me. I would even have to go to counseling. I needed a sounding board, a safe place to share my feelings. The Lord also used my pastor at the time in Brockton (who was white) minister to me. He challenged my thinking and taught me things that are with me to this day. He helped me to process some things and was a great help to me. I must add that had I not had the goal and desire to become an executive director, I would not have been so burdened. None of these things would have mattered if I had not wanted to advance, to go higher and be all that I could be in Christ, and for Christ.

While in counseling, I remember getting really frustrated with the counselor because, instead of giving me answers, he just kept asking me questions. It's like he wanted me to find the answer to my problem, which was that the race issue was too big for me to fix. It's been around since the beginning of time, and I can't change everything that needs changing.

At the time, I felt like some of the people (not all) who were telling me that Jesus loved me, also had their foot on my neck, keeping me down...keeping me from advancing. Some were dear white friends who I was very close to. My spirit was wounded when they told me that their child wanted to buy a black doll, but they couldn't make themselves do it. That hurt me and it confirmed my beliefs that they (some white people) felt they were superior. Then there was the white couple I had heard were fine with black people until one of them wanted to marry one of their children. This one always puzzled me...even now sometimes. Here is a praise report: I talked with my friends who initially did not want their daughter to have a black doll. Today, these many years later, we are the best of friends. Genuine and authentic friends!

In an earlier chapter, I mentioned that although I am very much Afrocentric and proud of my heritage and race, I have never been prejudice. I never allowed it to contaminate my soul. As most people know, the vast majority of black people are Democrats. Today, I'm a registered independent and have always been. I remember the early days in ministry when, because of comments made around me, I started to wonder if a Democrat could go to heaven! Of course, the answer is yes. To me, the people around me came across as if Jesus and His Father God were Republicans. When discussing politics, some of the things said I felt were offensive. I felt they were unloving and unchristian, too. Even today, political issues divide us.

My counseling ended successfully. I needed a neutral sounding board. I could share my feelings in a safe place. However, I will never forget how I got my breakthrough. The Lord reminded me of a speech that Dr. MLK, Jr. had made. In the speech, he had said if you sweep floors, then sweep them like Michelangelo painted pictures. I took this as God saying to me that whatever I am doing, I should do my best and do it to the glory of God. I got my breakthrough because I believe that God was telling me to move on and not to have anxiety about this issue of race, but to leave it in His hands.

I learned that He is sovereign and that if He opens a door, no one could shut it, and vice versa. Yes, people can slow you down and block you, but they cannot stop you...unless you allow them to. The Scriptures say, *"If God be for us, who can be against us?"* (Romans 8:31) I was giving white people too much credit. God is God all by Himself.

I used to not like a particular saying, but it is to be accepted as truth if we are going to believe in Jesus Christ and His Word. The saying that I used to hate to hear, but now I believe is, "We are all equal at the foot of the cross!"

After this premonition from the Lord, chains were broken. I had been set free. I had a new attitude. Then things started to turn in my favor. I would soon be appointed by the Southern New England Assemblies of God District to serve as the Executive of a new center that my wife and I were to pioneer in New Haven, Connecticut. It would be the very first Teen Challenge in the state of Connecticut. I was honored to be selected. I worked along the SNE District, the New Haven Steering Committee, and most importantly, with the Director of the Brockton Teen Challenge Center (Jim Vitale) who was from New Haven. The Brockton Center mothered the New Haven Center for two years while it got started. It was Jim Vitale's powerful testimony that led us in the direction of New Haven.

By the way, I've had both Christian counselors and secular counselors. I prefer Christian counseling every time, but it is not always needed. It depends on the issue. My very practical view and example I use is that if I were to fly in an airplane to China, which would I want? A Christian pilot or a non-Christian pilot? My answer? I want the one who is best at flying the airplane. Period.

Personally, I never experienced racism of any kind at Brooklyn Teen Challenge when I was going through the program. Since I have been around and involved with Teen Challenge, the Brooklyn Center has always seemed to have diversity. It's rare to see a lot of Afro Americans in a program. However, this does not mean anything sinister is happening.

Not too long ago, an East Coast Executive Director said to me, *"Floyd, black brothers are not coming here, and even if they come, they don't stay."* Don Wilkerson himself has publicly talked about this issue. He's personally dissatisfied by it. In my dad's autobiographical book (written almost fifty years ago), Dad said in the last chapter that there was a need for more black leaders in Teen Challenge. He shared how relieved black men were to see him on staff at the Brooklyn Center when they entered. Unfortunately, today things are not much different. The need is still there and this fact is coming from the top, and not just from me. There's no chip on my shoulder. As a matter of fact, I am exceedingly grateful to God for Teen Challenge. I'm a very proud card-carrying member in this organization. Yet, in my opinion, we can do better.

What about Brother Don Wilkerson having the entire men's program over to his house for Christmas? I was only two months in the program and being fresh out of Harlem, I was very skeptical and baffled as to why this white guy who did not know me or any of us would have us in his home? However, they showed nothing but genuine love and they even gave us meaningful gifts for Christmas, and not just trinkets.

A stronger commitment to the goal of producing more black and minority leaders is needed throughout Adult & Teen Challenges. There could even be centers in these black and/or diverse communities sponsored by other centers. Ever since I've been in Teen Challenge, I've always longed to see a center raised up in Harlem.

The current Teen Challenge organization that I'm a part of, with Dr. George Thomas (the President and CEO) has an excellent track record of raising up black leadership. Funny thing, there is no special program to do this. These men are just learning, putting in the work, and applying themselves after they graduate. They have a calling and their passion and heart's desire is to be servant leaders. Sort of like it was for me in my early days.

Ever since I was a student in Brooklyn, I wanted to be a Teen Challenge Director. No question, I didn't give the leaders any problems when I was in the program. I wanted to be like them. I set the bar high from the very beginning. When I was in Teen Challenge, I approached my learning as if I was in college. To my knowledge, in 1982 there were not any black executive directors that I knew of. If any, there may have been a few program directors; but that's all. In my heart of hearts as I looked around the country at the landscape of what I saw, I did not truly feel, believe, or accept that this was God's will. It would even offend me if someone was to suggest this to me at the time. I would hear people say that things will change in God's time. However, I felt that I was too smart to believe that. To me, that sounded ridiculous. I believed that there were not any Afro American executive directors, etc. because this is the way that they wanted it. It was intentional. Why? Because if the commitment was there, things would be different. In my mind, I was saying that drugs and alcohol affect black and brown people disproportionately. It only made sense to me that more blacks should be in leadership. Amen?

I look back over my life of being a Teen Challenge graduate, leader and an ordained A/G minister... (which by the way, is a great fellowship that I am very proud to be a part of). Teen Challenge is the world's most effective Christian organization of its kind. It wouldn't hurt if more effort, commitment, and resources are put towards having more blacks and minorities raised up as future leaders. I personally know how a little encouragement in this area can go a long way. For example, when I was a fairly new minister, I attended the A/G Inner City Worker's Conference, in New Orleans, LA. (It is now called the Black Assemblies of God). The founder and president (Bishop Spencer Jones) had paid for all my expenses to attend without even knowing me. I was ministering in New England at the time and had heard about this group comprised of African American churches, sanctioned by the A/G District & National Leadership. There were other nationalities present as well...red, yellow, black and white. Bishop Jones had invited me to come after I shared my heart over the phone about some of the things I was feeling and seeing throughout New England along with my struggles as a credential holder in the A/G.

Long story short: When I entered, the conference's praise and worship service (conducted in our native tradition) felt and sounded so awesome and beautiful. I recall not being able to make it past the fifth row as I sat down and began to weep. Why was I weeping? Maybe it was because I felt safe and valued. Sort of like, I finally made it back home. I'll never forget all the sharp, bright and anointed African American brothers and sisters teaching the workshops and preaching; all bona fide leaders! Wow! That was exactly what I needed to see. That was the missing link. This was scarce in New England and in the A/G at the time. Today, by the grace of God, we've come a long way and are headed in the right direction.

I don't have to attend every Black A/G conference today. I go when I can or when I need to. I'm very comfortable in my skin and don't need to travel halfway across the country to get my "black on." However, it's good to know they are there. Furthermore, my wife and I are in a church with 25-plus nationalities; a small glimpse of what heaven will be like!

11
Moving Forward

As I look back, I can't help but marvel at how faithful God has been to me (and continues to be), and how He has fulfilled my God-given desire to serve Him in leadership roles. Also, I can see that all my life long God has (and continues) to love me through others. I'm grateful that the Lord enabled me to see with my own eyes the dramatic transformation of my dad (even though he was not perfect). And yet, that wasn't quite enough to initially convince me of my need for a Savior. It was God who used the Teen Challenge counselor to show me my self-centered perspective and selfish lifestyle. That was the spiritual breakthrough which opened my eyes to my personal need for Christ. Since then, God has redeemed the sorrows and pains of my past by equipping me and using me as an agent of healing to many other hurting people.

By the grace of God, my future is bright because the God who was and is, will always be faithful, loving, and redemptive. Romans 8:28 says that ALL things work together for good to those who love God and those who are called according to His purpose. Dear Reader, do you truly and wholeheartedly love God? We love Him because He first loved us. He first loved us by dying on the cross for us all. That sacrificial act demands our attention: JESUS DIED FOR YOU, after all! When we give that our attention, Christ then wins our affection, and we too become lovers of God! If you haven't done so, why don't you stop right now, say a prayer and ask Christ to be your Savior right now. He will hear and answer you, too...just like he answered me when I cried out to Him when I was living in that abandoned building in Harlem.

Before I end this book, I want to very humbly but boldly let you know of what God, by His mercy, has been able to accomplish through me. This is not to puff me up or to be prideful. I am nothing without God, but I want to encourage those in need of hope (along with all the Teen Challenge readers) to go higher than me and to progress even more.

By the grace of God, I've earned an undergraduate and a graduate degree. I'm an ordained Assemblies of God minister and a licensed chemical dependency counselor. I have served as a lead pastor with my wife and children by my side helping me. I was appointed by my leaders to start the first Teen Challenge in Connecticut, and I have served on many boards. Once again, the only reason I share this is so that the men and women coming up behind me can know and thus be able to dream and get a vision from the Lord to be used mightily by Him.

My best days are still ahead of me and I am not looking at life through a rearview mirror! Today I'm excited about the assignment God has me on at the Adult & Teen Challenge of Texas. Our President and CEO, Dr. George Thomas, has a wonderful vision that I'm blessed to have been brought into. This organization has six adult men programs, two adult women programs, an adolescent program for girls and one for boys. Also, we have a women and children's program and one for women being rescued from sex trafficking.

By the grace of God, I have been on several foreign missionary trips to launch and/or help a Teen Challenge Center in other countries. Specifically, I have travelled to Africa four times, Fiji, Jamaica, Scotland, and the Bahamas, etc. When my wife and I traveled to Israel with a group of ministers, we stayed at the same hotel of the late evangelist Morris Cerullo. As I mentioned earlier, God supernaturally had given Mr. Cerullo a Word of Knowledge about me when I responded to an altar call as a student in Teen Challenge. The word from Dr. Cerullo confirmed to me that I was to go to Bible school instead of the Armed Forces. Thankfully, I was able to share that story with Mr. Cerullo at the hotel.

Perhaps, you are reading this and you're able to identify with this story and some of the things I have experienced and described. Well, let me just tell you, they are not coincidences. God is real and He is calling you. There isn't any doubt that I can look back on my life and see God protecting and guiding me every step of the way. He allowed me to live because He had a purpose for me. My test(s) became my testimony, to the glory of God!

All that I have done and been a part of has been a huge honor and privilege. I'm currently a Bible teacher, an elder, and a "Celebrate Recovery" leader at Bethel Covenant Assemblies of God in San Antonio, led by Rev. Drs. John and Chidi Aniemeke. By the way, thank God for live streaming, but Church attendance and involvement is God's will for everyone! This is particularly important for the Teen Challenge student and graduate because they are not naturally and automatically disciplined to do this. Unfortunately today, many people go church hopping in the same way they use to go nightclub hopping. That is not good. The church and pastor must take over as "the spiritual covering" after a person graduates from Teen Challenge.

As a matter of fact, it is God's will for every believer to attend church and have a pastor. Jesus is the Head of the church, and serving in His church and fellowshipping with the body of Christ is the only way that people in general and/or TC graduates can grow properly and continue to mature. Hebrews 10:24 says, *"Let us hold fast the profession of our faith without wavering; (for He is faithful that promised). And let us consider one another to provoke unto love and to good works: not forsaking the assembling of ourselves together, as the manner of some is; but exhorting one another: and so much the more, as ye see the day approaching."*

Prior to our conversion, we frequented ungodly places and many of our friends were involved in ungodly things, too. Well, God has brought us out of that lifestyle and we mustn't return. 1 Peter 2:9 declares that, *"You are a chosen people, a royal priesthood, a holy nation, God's special possession that you may declare the praises of Him who called you out of darkness into His wonderful light."* Let's continue to declare God's praises as He continues to call people out of darkness and into the light of the Gospel (the good news) of Christ.

There is so much more that needs to be done, especially among the African American communities. As Rev. Don Wilkerson, Co-Founder of Teen Challenge and Times Square Church said in the Foreword, *"It's my prayer that this book can prompt a discussion of how to increase outreach evangelism to drug addicts and alcoholics everywhere—but especially among African Americans, beginning in Harlem and beyond."*

In my dad's autobiography, *Black Tracts*, written nearly fifty years ago, he told of how he was delivered from a nineteen-year heroin addiction in thirty seconds when he cried out to Jesus. Ironically, in the last chapter of his book, he also mentioned the need for more African Americans in Teen Challenge. My lifelong dream, vision, and prayer is to see Teen Challenge (the world's most effective Christian drug program) in Central Harlem one day...the place of my birth, the place of my beginnings, and the place that I love. It is very much needed there! May the Almighty God who gives us visions and dreams make those visions and dreams come true. Join me in prayer that the Lord would raise up a Teen Challenge Center in Harlem one day, for the honor and glory of His name!

"Now to him who is able to do
immeasurably more than all we ask or imagine,
according to his power that is at work within us,
to him be glory in the church and in Christ Jesus
throughout all generations,
for ever and ever!
Amen."
(Ephesians 3:20, 21, NIV)

Top to Bottom: Tia and her Kid's Graduation;
Floyd's Father; Floyd at the age of 8.

Top Left to Right: Family Gathering; Rev. Miles speaking; Family Portrait; New Orleans Teen Challenge; Floyd and Mary.

Top Left to Right: Floyd's Grandmother; Wedding Day; Floyd and
Glenda, his first cousin; Floyd's Father at Teen Challenge;
The abandoned building Floyd lived in.

Top Left to Right: Rev. Miles & Mary in Africa;
Rev. Miles teaching in Africa; Floyd IV and Tyler;
Preaching to Kids in Jamaica;

Top Left to Right: Floyd and Son at Sylvia's in Harlem; Floyd's Mother; Floyd (right) and Harlem Buddies; Soul Saving Station in Harlem.

Our 25th Anniversary Renewal of Vows; Floyd, Wife & Daughter in front of famed Apollo; Floyd & Rev. Joe Paskewich with Pastor Carter Colon of Times Square Church; Grandchildren Nylah & Kamani; Sister Denise.

Top Left to Right: Family Portrait; New Hampshire College Graduation; Victory Christian Center Congregation in Indiana; Pastor Floyd and Stepmom Barbara and Sister; Major Donation to Texas TC.

Top Left to Right: Floyd Miles IV, Marine; Floyd's Mom;
With Rev. Dr. John and Chidi Aniemeke; At TC Banquet.

ENDNOTES

[i] Https://www.brainyquote.com/quotes/teyana_taylor_510829.

[ii] Brown, Claude. *Manchild in the Promised Land.* United Kingdom, Scribner, 2012, p. 394.

[iii] Https://www.brainyquote.com/quotes/kareem_abduljabbar_467148

[iv] Https://www.azquotes.com/quote/1530870

[v] Https://www.azquotes.com/quote/1144813

[vi] Speech at Founding Rally of the Organization of Afro-American Unity (28 June 1964) As quoted in *By Any Means Necessary.* Atlanta, Pathfinder Press, 1970.

[vii] Davis, Ossie. *With Ossie and Ruby: In This Life Together.* New York, It Books, 2000, p. 64.

[viii] www.brainyquote.com › Authors › Colin Powell Quotes

[ix] King, Jr., Martin Luther. *The Last Interview and Other Conversations by Martin Luther.* Brooklyn, Melville House, 2007, p. 70.

[x] *Take the 'A' Train,* Written by: Billy Strayhorn, BMG Rights Management.

[xi] Fox, Ted. *Showtime at the Apollo.* New York, Harry N. Abrams, 2003.

[xii] *Deposing 'King Heroin'* from Dear Abby. Sun-Sentinel, https://www.sun-sentinel.com/news/fl-xpm-1997-02-25-9702240120-story.html.

About Adult & Teen Challenge

For over sixty years, Adult & Teen Challenge has operated on a holistic model of drug and alcohol recovery. This means that we are concerned with the body, mind, and spirit of those who come to our addiction recovery centers. Our vision is to see all people freed from addiction through the power of Jesus Christ!

A restored relationship with God can transform those who suffer from addiction into vibrant, free, and sober followers of the Lord. We base the curriculum and community of our addiction recovery centers on God's Word—the Bible. Our practical Bible-based courses help the transition from alcoholism and substance abuse to a life of freedom in Christ. We offer a chance to start over, become a new person, live a godly life, and find freedom through a restored purpose and an eternal hope. This is done through classes, individual study, personal mentoring, work ethic training, and involvement in the Christian community.

There are over 200 Adult & Teen Challenge residential programs throughout the United States. All offer a variety of services that provide help for people struggling with drugs, alcohol, and other life controlling issues. Admission requirements, fees, and tuition costs vary from program to program. As a 501© (3), we are dedicated to providing cost-effective programs. However, there are many costs involved in providing training, lodging, meals, supervision. These expenses require the generous support of our friends, faith communities, and society.

Because addiction destroys more than the body, our programs consider all aspects of our students' lives. Addiction starts as a way to fulfill a void that only God can fill, so a strong relationship with the Lord is foundational to our program. This foundation is built in our students by teaching them the Word of God and by encouraging them to bond with other growing disciples.

Taken from https://teenchallengeusa.org/about/

Our History

Led by incredible faith, David Wilkerson made a seemingly bizarre step from his country pulpit in 1958 to the streets of New York City, where a murder trial of seven teenage boys churned society's antipathy toward them. Even Wilkerson was bewildered by his sense of compassion but, in spite of doubt, he followed the Spirit's prompting to help the boys.

Wilkerson's outreach to gangs in New York led to the development of Teen Challenge. From our simple beginnings, Teen Challenge has grown to over 200 locations in the US and over 1000 around the world. The explosive growth of Teen Challenge continues to be a true move of God.

Taken from https://teenchallengeusa.org/history/

About the Author

After successfully completing Teen Challenge, Floyd went to college, seminary, and became an Assemblies of God minister. Floyd has been giving back, working with men and women with drug and alcohol problems for over thirty years. Rev. Miles is a licensed Chemical Dependency Counselor and a certified Mental Health Coach. He and his lovely wife Mary Miles have been happily married for nearly thirty-six years. They have four children (Tia, Jea'na, Floyd IV and Tyler) and five grandchildren (Cassidy, Cody, Nylah, Kamani and Kenzie).

floydmiles1618@gmail.com

https://www.facebook.com/floyd.amilesiii

Brooklyn Teen Challenge's website is: www.brooklyntc.org

Adult & Teen Challenge of Texas' Website is:
https://teenchallengetx.org/

Printed in Great Britain
by Amazon

52638431R00077